Perceptions of Title IX's impact on gender equity within intercollegiate athletics: The Mississippi public community and junior colleges

By

Roderick Van Daniel

A Dissertation
Submitted to the Faculty of
Mississippi State University
in Partial Fulfillment of the Requirements
for the Degree of Doctor of Philosophy
inCommunity College Leadership
in the Department of Leadership and Foundations

Mississippi State, Mississippi

December 2012

Copyright by

Roderick Van Daniel

2012

Perceptions of Title IX's impact on gender equity within intercollegiate

athletics: The Mississippi public community and junior colleges

By

Roderick Van Daniel

Approved:

_____
Debra L. Prince
Associate Professor of
Leadership and Foundations
(Director of Dissertation)

_____
James E. Davis
Associate Professor of
Leadership and Foundations
(Committee Member)

_____
William M. Wiseman
Professor of Political and Public
Administration
(Committee Member)

_____
Megan E. Holmes
Assistant Professor of Kinesiology
(Committee Member)

_____
R. Dwight Hare
Professor and Graduate Coordinator of
Leadership and Foundations
(Committee Member)

_____
Richard Blackbourn
Dean of College of Education

Name: Roderick Van Daniel

Date of Degree: December 15, 2012

Institution: Mississippi State University

Major Field: Community College Leadership

Major Professor: Dr. Debra L. Prince

Title of Study:  Perceptions of Title IX's impact on gender equity within intercollegiate athletics: The Mississippi public community and junior colleges

Pages in Study: 85

Candidate for Degree of Doctor of Philosophy

Title IX's legislation has been in place since 1972 and has affected female participation in a positive form towards gender equity. However many institution still have difficulty complying with the standards mandated by Title IX. Gender equity is established by meeting substantial proportionality, continued expansion, or full accommodations prongs mandated by Title IX for an institution to be in compliance.

The purpose of this study was to determine the perceptions of the athletic directors of the 15 public community and junior colleges in Mississippi regarding Title IX compliance and determine if their respective institutions are in compliance with the substantial proportionality (SP) prong of Title IX. The study identified the perceptions of the athletic directors regarding their institutions' Title IX compliance, as well as the effective strategies and barriers toward meeting the requirements to comply with Title IX within their programs. In addition, the study revealed whether or not the institutions complied with the SP prong of Title IX.

Athletic directors (N=15; 53% response rate) from the public community and junior colleges from Mississippi completed the Two-Year College Title IX Survey.

Results revealed that overall the athletic directors perceived that their institutions were in compliance with Title IX. However, the athletic directors perceived that the listed strategies were not effective and the barriers listed were not perceived barriers to Title IX compliance. However, the Equity in Athletics Disclosure Act data revealed that none of the institutions complied with the SP prong of Title IX. From a practical perspective, the study revealed that while the athletic directors perceived that their institutions met the SP prong, EADA data revealed that none of the institutions in the state met that prong. Consequently, this finding indicates that there is a need for more education regarding Title IX compliance at the institutions. This information could serve as a starting point for an in-depth institutional study on Title IX. From a theoretical perspective, the study provided information that gives leaders at the public community and junior colleges in Mississippi a unique look at diversity within their athletic departments.

# DEDICATION

This research is dedicated to my mother, Yvonne Daniel, for listening to my dreams, encouraging me to achieve my goals, and providing the support for me to be strong. Mom, you have inspired me from the moment you gave birth to me. I love you. You instilled in me the importance of education but more importantly to graduate with the degree. Thanks for always encouraging me to keep the Lord with me on my educational journey and in my everyday life. Mom, thank you for the financial support. I never would have made it without you. I love you so much.

This research is also dedicated to my brothers, Dashmond and Zerdock, sister, Ashalond Daniel, and my father Roy Garth. You gave me strength each day. Thank you for believing that dreams do come true; I did it!

To my grandmother, Clara Betts Daniel, thank you for instilling the Lord in my life. I miss you. Thank you for telling me that I have to be strong to survive in this world. Thank you for telling me to hold my head up high and not walk with it down. Thank you for making me come inside the house before the street lights came on at night. I want to thank you for loving me and telling me that you have to leave the nest sometimes to truly become the man that you desire to become. Thank you for telling me to carry the Lord's scripture in my pocket every day, "The Lord is my shepard; I shall not want." I thank you for being strong; you made me strong through being around you. You lived to be in your nineties; you gave me wisdom and strength beyond my childhood years. I miss you. I love you still. Only the strong survive, you told me to remember that always. I stand strong for you and my family. I thank you.

Thank you God and Jesus for I can do all things because the strengthen me. Thanks for making me strong in your word and truth; I love you both.

## ACKNOWLEDGEMENTS

First and foremost, I acknowledge Jesus and God for being instrumental in my life. I would not be in the position to accomplish my dreams without either of them. Secondly, I acknowledge the members of my dissertation committee, Dr. Ed Davis, Dr. Marty Wiseman, Dr. Megan Holmes, and Dr. Dwight Hare. Lastly but most importantly, I acknowledge my dissertation chair, Dr. Debra Prince. She gave me strength when I needed help from all the aspects of my educational and life journey towards attaining the doctorate of philosophy degree. She has been my mentor for way longer than she ever knew. Truly, I am blessed for having you in my life; the Lord puts certain people in your life for a reason. It has been a true blessing having you guide me into being a better man on my educational and life journey.

TABLE OF CONTENTS

DEDICATION .................................................................................................... ii

ACKNOWLEDGEMENTS ................................................................................ iv

LIST OF TABLES ............................................................................................ vii

CHAPTER

    I.    INTRODUCTION ....................................................................................1

           Statement of Problem.................................................................3
           Purpose of Study ........................................................................4
           Research Questions ....................................................................5
           Theoretical Framework..............................................................5
           Justification for Study ................................................................6
           Delimitations..............................................................................7
           Limitations .................................................................................8
           Definition of Terms...................................................................8
           Summary ....................................................................................9

    II.    LITERATURE REVIEW ........................................................................11

           Overview of the Mississippi Public Community and Junior Colleges ............12
           Title IX and Intercollegiate Athletics .....................................13
           Empirical Evidence and Title IX .............................................18
                Examination of Title IX Compliance..........................18
                Perception of Title IX Compliance.............................22
           Summary ..................................................................................27

    III.    METHODOLOGY .................................................................................28

           Research Design.......................................................................28
           Participants...............................................................................29
           Instruments...............................................................................30
                Two Year Institution Title IX Survey.........................30
                      validity and reliability ....................................31
                EADA Survey .............................................................33
           Procedures................................................................................34

|  |  | Data Analysis | 34 |
|---|---|---|---|
|  |  | Summary | 36 |
| IV. | RESULTS | | 37 |
|  |  | Demographics | 37 |
|  |  | Research Question 1 | 38 |
|  |  | Research Question 2 | 40 |
|  |  | Research Question 3 | 44 |
|  |  | Research Question 4 | 50 |
|  |  | Summary | 51 |
| V. | SUMMARY, DISCUSSION, AND RECOMMENDATIONS | | 53 |
|  |  | Summary | 53 |
|  |  | Discussion | 56 |
|  |  | Recommendations | 61 |
|  |  | Institutional Recommendations | 61 |
|  |  | Research Recommendations | 63 |

REFERENCES ................................................................................................................65

APPENDIX

| A. | SURVEY APPROVAL LETTER | 71 |
|---|---|---|
| B. | TWO YEAR INSTITUTION TITLE IX SURVEY | 73 |
| C. | IRB APPROVAL LETTER | 84 |

## LIST OF TABLES

| | | |
|---|---|---|
| Table 1 | Mississippi Public Community and Junior Colleges | 13 |
| Table 2 | Perceptions of Senior Women Athletic Administrators Regarding Specific Areas of Title IX Compliance | 23 |
| Table 3 | Perceptions of Title IX Compliance Results | 40 |
| Table 4 | Number and Percentage of Item Choice Selections | 43 |
| Table 5 | Strategies to Strengthen Title IX Compliance Results | 44 |
| Table 6 | Number and Percentage of Item Choice Selections | 47 |
| Table 7 | Barriers to Title IX Compliance Results | 49 |
| Table 8 | Title IX SP Compliance by Institution | 51 |

CHAPTER I

INTRODUCTION

In the United States, community colleges are essential in the educational landscape of the country; over 40% of all undergraduates in the country are enrolled in community colleges (American Association of Community Colleges [AACC], 2012). According to the AACC, one of the distinctive features of community colleges is their accessibility to women. In 2012, AACC stated that 57% of the 12 million students enrolled in community colleges were women. Community colleges also play a considerable part in providing opportunities for students to participate in athletic programs. According to Brawer and Cohen (2003), community colleges are the institutions of choice for many more students to further their education and their athletic aspirations. However, similar to other aspects of society, the opportunities afforded men and women have not always been equitable in education or athletics (Burgess, 2005).

In the 1970s when the civil rights period began to expand its focus more toward the injustices, rights, and concerns of women and other minorities, scholarly interest was directed toward the impact of Title IX of the Education Amendment Act of 1972 on gender equity (Ward, 2004). Title IX of the Education Amendment Act of 1972, according to Mumford (2006), was passed to strengthen the impact of Title VII of the Civil Rights Act of 1964, which stated that employees could not discriminate on the basis of race, color, religion, sex or national origin. In 1972, Title IX extended that same philosophy to any program that received funding from the federal government (Eckes & Chamberlin, 2003). As stated in the Title IX legislation, "No person in the United States shall, on the basis of sex, be excluded from participation in, be denied the benefits of, or be subjected to discrimination under any educational program or activity receiving federal financial assistance" (United States Department of Justice [USDJ], 2001, p. 7). Consequently, Title IX required equal opportunities for students in all educational activities including athletics (Compton, Compton, Dawe, & Dawe, 2007).

Title IX compliance is directed to all the public educational programs. However, intercollegiate athletics has been the focus of attention due to gender inequality in the area of student athletic participation (Anderson, Cheslock, & Ehrenberg, 2006). While Title IX has removed many of the barriers that once inhibited individuals on the basis of sex, from participating in athletic, educational, and career opportunities (USDJ, 2001), according to Stafford (2004), the majority of public colleges and universities are still not in compliance with Title IX. For example, a study published in 2004 examined Title IX compliance in California's public high schools, community colleges, and universities found major gender discrepancies in all three sectors (Beam, Faddis, & Ruzicka, 2004). According to the Beam et al., the vast majority of high schools, community colleges, and universities in California failed to meet Title IX compliance standards. Mumford (2005) found similar results when he examined gender equity in the community colleges in the state of Maryland. According to Mumford, although women represented 61% of the enrollment in Maryland's community colleges, they only represented 32% of the athletic population. Consequently, by Title IX standards, this gap of 29 percentage points is unacceptable. Despite the many gains in opportunities made available to women in both education and athletics, the gap identified by Mumford indicates that there is still cause for concern in regards to Title IX compliance.

## Statement of the Problem

Since the passage of Title IX, significant progress has been made in issues of gender equity in intercollegiate athletic programs (Schneider, Stier, Henry, & Wilding, 2010). In fact, according to Lipka (2007), the athletic opportunities available to women were higher in 2007 than they had ever been. However, to say that most educational institutions are in compliance with Title IX would be inaccurate. As stated by Schneider et al. (2010), "Resistance, in some circles, to gender equity in athletic departments is a 'constant' as is evident in the numerous Title IX infractions that have been formally documented since the law's establishment" (p.104). The notion of resistance to issues of gender equity is a well-documented problem in 4-year colleges and universities throughout the nation (Causby, 2010). However, the primary issue that supported theneed for the current study was the paucity of literature on gender equity in communitycollege athletic programs. There is very little empirical research documenting resistance to issues of gender equity in community college populations. An assumption held by this researcher is that there is also resistance to issues of gender equity in the community college sector. Moreover, similar to the findings of Cook (2010) who found a gap between the factual knowledge of Title IX and the perceptions of the law amongst leaders at institutions of higher learning, an assumption held by this researcher is that the gap exists amongst leaders of the community and junior colleges in

Mississippi. Despite Title IX's mandate for gender equity more than 40 years ago, overcoming barriers to female athletic participation still remains a challenging problem nationwide (Hoffman, 2010).

## Purpose of the Study

Although Title IX was enacted over 40 years ago, institutions receiving federal funds still find achieving and maintaining gender equity in athletics to be a challenge (Cheslock & Eckes, 2008; Hoffman, 2010; Schneider et al., 2010). To address this challenge, it is imperative that accurate depictions of the current status of Title IX compliance are known (Schneider et al., 2010). The purpose of this study was to determine the perceptions of the athletic directors of the 15 public community and junior colleges in Mississippi regarding Title IX compliance and to determine if their respective institutions are in compliance with the Substantial Proportionality (SP) prong of Title IX. SP is determined by comparing the percentage of women in the athletic program to the percentage of women in the overall, full-time student population (Campbell, 2010; Staurowsky, 2009). To be in compliance with the SP prong, the difference between the percentage of females represented in the overall athletic population and the percentage of females represented in the institution's population must not exceed five percentage points.

**Research Questions**

This study focused on the gender equity clause of the Title IX legislation at community and junior colleges in the state of Mississippi. To fulfill the purpose of this research, the following research questions were developed and answered:

1. What are the perceptions of the athletic directors of Mississippi's public community and junior colleges regarding their institution's level of Title IX compliance?

2. What are the perceptions of the athletic directors of Mississippi's public community and junior colleges regarding the effectiveness of specific strategies to strengthen Title IX compliance efforts at their respective institutions?

3. What are the perceptions of the athletic directors of Mississippi's public community and junior colleges regarding barriers to Title IX compliance at their respective institutions?

4. Are the public community and junior colleges in the state of Mississippi in compliance with the SP prong of Title IX?

**Theoretical framework**

The primary legal struggle over Title IX compliance in athletics has been the understanding of Title IX as it pertains to increasing opportunities for women in the arena of competitive sports (Brake, 2001). Therefore, the impetus for this study was grounded in not only equality for women but also the means of establishing equality through law. Consequently, the theoretical framework that supports this study is that of the feminist legal theory.

The feminist legal theory suggests that laws and institutions must be continually examined as understanding and knowledge increases to satisfy the goal of equality for women (Hunter, 2012). According to Hunter, even in the aspect of laws, women have not always received equal or fair treatment. In athletics, as in other areas of feminist concern, there is tension among feminist scholars about how best to respond to conditions of inequality and the resulting difference in treatment between men and women in society (Brake, 2001). According to Bartlett and Kennedy (1992), appropriate responses to issues of inequality can only be accomplished through interpreting relationships between the statute (i.e. Title IX) and gender equality.

## Justification for Study

Two overlapping themes provided the justification for this study. The first theme was the significance of community and junior colleges in the educational landscape of the American educational system. According to Causby (2010), over 12 million students are enrolled in community and junior colleges throughout the nation. Furthermore, females represent the majority enrollment of those community and junior colleges. That being the case, accurate descriptions of different aspects of community and junior colleges in the nation provides needed snapshots of the American higher educational system.

The second theme that provided justification for this study is grounded in the significance of Title IX. As stated by Campbell (2010), since the passage of Title IX, the number of females participating in intercollegiate sports has increased dramatically. However, the author acknowledged that there is still much improvement needed. This need for improvement and the potential sanctions for not improving justified the need for this study. According to the Title IX, any coeducational institution with an athletic program receiving federal funds must comply with Title IX or risk the loss of federalfunds. Consequently, the decision makers and leaders of Mississippi's community and junior colleges can use the results of this study as they work to achieve or maintain compliance with Title IX and not jeopardize federal funding.

Moreover, a review of the literature did not reveal any studies examining gender equity in athletics in Mississippi's public community and junior colleges. Because all of these institutions offer intercollegiate athletic programs, gender equity and Title IX should be a legitimate concern for the leaders of these institutions. A statewide perspective provides valuable information to the leaders of the Mississippi Association of Community and Junior Colleges (MACJC) as well as member institutions by describing the strategies and barriers athletic directors identified with respect to gender equity and Title IX compliance. Moreover, a thorough examination of student participation rates provided a first step in enabling the leaders to develop or refine their systematic plans to ensure Title IX compliance.

**Delimitations**

1. This study was limited to the 15 public community and junior colleges in the state of Mississippi. It is not the intent of this study to generalize to any other community or junior college system.
2. The study was limited to the responses of athletic directors at the 15 public community and junior colleges in the state of Mississippi and not the views of other administrators, coaches, or student-athletes.

3. The study was limited to public two-year institutions versus private two-year institutions.

## Limitations

1. This study utilized data recorded in the online Equity in Athletics Data Analysis Cutting Tool from the United State Department of Education. In which case, this study may be limited by the accuracy of data recorded.
2. This study utilized data gathered from a survey and is limited by the truthfulness of the respondents.
3. The overall response rate for the Two Year Institution Title IX Survey was 53% (eight of 15 athletic directors responded). Moreover, of the eight respondents, only five athletic directors completed the entire survey. Consequently, the interpretations of the results of the data analysis are limited.

## Definition of Terms

The following terms represent common terms that are relevant to this study:

1. *Athletic Director* - the person who attends public relations and fund-raising events, participates in negotiating contracts, and the representative for the interests of the athletic department in the development of institutional policies and financial affairs (Barr, Hums, & Masteralexis, 2005).
2. *Athletically-related student aid* - any scholarship, grant, or other form of financial assistance, offered by an institution which require the recipient to participate in a

program of intercollegiate athletics at the institution (United States Department of Education, 2009).

3. *Community College* - sometimes referred to as a junior college, is any educational institution regionally accredited to award the associate in arts or the associate in science as its highest degree (Cohen & Brawer, 2003).

4. *Compliance* - the adherence to NJCAA, National Collegiate Athletic Association and conference rules and regulations; the compliance coordinator in an athletic department is responsible for educating coaches and student-athletes about the rules and regulations, overseeing the initial and continuing eligibility of student-athletes, and preventing or investigating any violations that occur (Barr et al., 2005).

5. *Equality* - the quality or state of being equal (Webster's Dictionary, 2007).

6. *Equity* - the fairness or justice in dealings between persons (Webster's Dictionary, 2007).

7. *Student-Athlete* - an individual who chooses to participate in both the academic and athletic environment of a selected educational institution (Burgess, 2005).

**Summary**

The purpose of this study was to determine the perceptions of the athletic directors of Mississippi's public community and junior colleges regarding Title IX compliance and to determine if the community and junior colleges in Mississippi were in compliance with the SP prong of Title IX. This dissertation was organized into five chapters. Chapter I provided an introduction to the study and included the statement of the problem, the purpose of the study, the research questions, the theoretical frame, the justification for the study, and the study's limitations and delimitations. Chapter I also included a definition of terms. Chapter II provided a review of the literature that informed the study and Chapter III presented the methodology that was used to conduct the study. Chapter IV presented the results of the analysis of data that was used to answer the research questions and Chapter V presented a discussion of those results and offers recommendations based on those results.

CHAPTER II

LITERATURE REVIEW

Title IX and gender equity are exceptionally sensitive subjects in education and athletics. In the early 1970s, gender equity became a major political issue in the United States. Nowhere was this more evident than in the educational system, particularly in the movement for women to participate in intercollegiate athletics (Causby, 2010). The purpose of the present study was to determine the perceptions of the athletic directors of the 15 public community and junior colleges in Mississippi regarding Title IX compliance and to determine if their respective institutions are in compliance with the SP prong of Title IX. This chapter, Chapter II, provides a review of the literature that informed this study and is organized into four main sections. First, the review includes a brief description and discussion of the public community and junior colleges in Mississippi. Then the review provides background information on the Title IX legislation as it relates to intercollegiate athletics. The third section of the review discusses empirical evidence related to Title IX compliance and the final section provides a summary of the literature reviewed and the gaps in the literature that this study was designed to fill.

## Overview of Mississippi's Public Community and Junior Colleges

Mississippi was the first state in the nation to establish a system of public community and junior colleges (Fatheree, 2012). The Mississippi public community and junior college system began in 1922 with the passage of Senate Bill No. 251, introduced by Dr. Julius Christian Zeller, a senator from Yazoo County, Mississippi (Young & Ewing, 1978). As introduced, community and junior colleges were to provide a quality, accessible, and inexpensive education for students in Mississippi. According to Senate Bill No. 251, to avoid competition with universities, a community or junior college had to be, at a minimum, 20 miles from the University of Mississippi in Oxford, Mississippi State University in Starkville, Mississippi University for Women in Columbus, and the University of Southern Mississippi in Hattiesburg (Fatheree, 2012). As a result of this legislation, and in the same year that the legislation passed, two of the state's fifty agricultural high schools extended their curricula to include the studies of the freshman year of college work (Young & Ewing, 1978). Pearl River Agricultural High School in Poplarville and Hinds County Agricultural High School in Raymond offered college courses in the fall semester of 1922 (Fatheree, 2012). During that semester, Pearl River Agricultural High School enrolled 13 students and Hinds County Agricultural High School enrolled 30 students (Young & Ewing, 1978). Six years later, Mississippi had 10 agricultural high schools that offering at least one year of college courses (Fatheree, 2012).

Mississippi presently has 14 community colleges and one junior college. All of these institutions provide educational services and programs that are accessible to practically any Mississippi citizen (State Board for Community and Junior Colleges

[SBCJC], 2012). Mississippi's public community and junior colleges are funded by state appropriations, local district taxes, student fees, and federal grants and offer both university transfer credit and occupational programs (SBCJC, 2012). Moreover, all of the community or junior colleges have intercollegiate athletic programs. Table 1 displays the 2010-2011 enrollment data and institution location data retrieved from The Integrated Postsecondary Education Data System (IPEDS, 2012) for each of the 15 institutions.

Table 1

Mississippi Public Community and Junior Colleges

| Institution | Enrollment | Location |
| --- | --- | --- |
| Coahoma Community College | 2,379 | Clarksdale |
| Copiah-Lincoln Community College | 3,213 | Wesson |
| East Central Community College | 2,189 | Decatur |
| East Mississippi Community College | 2,954 | Scooba |
| Hinds Community College | 9,820 | Raymond |
| Holmes Community College | 4,577 | Goodman |
| Itawamba Community College | 5,757 | Fulton |
| Jones County | 4,081 | Ellisville |
| Meridian Community College | 2,945 | Meridian |
| Mississippi Delta Community College | 2,397 | Moorhead |
| Mississippi Gulf Coast Community College | 6,989 | Perkinston |
| Northeast Mississippi | 3,099 | Booneville |
| Northwest Mississippi Community College | 5,189 | Senatobia |
| Pearl River Community College | 4,019 | Poplarville |
| Southwest Mississippi Community College | 1,572 | Summit |

**Title IX and Intercollegiate Athletics**

In an attempt to stop gender discrimination in education, women's rights advocates sought political and governmental solutions to influence change in the structure of education in the United States. Modeled after Title VII of the Civil Rights Act of 1964, which prohibits employment discrimination on the basis of race and gender, Title IX was enacted to fight against injustices to women in all federally funded programs

(Passeggi, 2002). According to the Title IX legislation enacted in 1972, "No person in the United States shall, on the basis of sex, be excluded from participation in, be denied the benefits of, or be subjected to discrimination under any education program or activity receiving federal financial assistance" (USDJ, 2001, p. 7). Former Senator Birch Bayh of Indiana sponsored the bill in the United States Senate stating that economic inequalities are directly related to the educational inequalities suffered by women (USDJ, 2001). Consequently, Senator Bayh believed a strong legal mechanism was needed to protect women from discrimination in educational institutions. Prior to 1972 when Title IX was enacted, a true injustice existed for women in terms of educational and athletic opportunities. According to Vest and Masterson (2007), women were often treated as second-class citizens in academics and athletics. Before the passage of Title IX, fewer than 30,000 women participated in intercollegiate athletics (Campbell, 2010). Consequently, Title IX put the force of law behind the reality that women were entitled to fairness and equality.

Although the statute was not enacted specifically for intercollegiate athletics, Title IX affected female participation in athletics in dramatic form. Much of the significance attributed to Title IX compliance, as it relates to providing athletic opportunities to women, is associated with increased educational opportunities. According to Mumford (2006), athletic scholarships often provide means of attending college for women who would otherwise not be able to afford postsecondary education. As a result of the enactment of Title IX, the opportunities for women to participate in intercollegiate athletics increased tremendously (Mumford, 2006). By 2003, the number of women participating in intercollegiate athletics had escalated to slightly over 200,000 (Campbell, 2010). According to the National Women's Law Center (2002), intercollegiate athletics have not been the same since the implementation of Title IX in 1972. However, inequalities in athletic participations rates are still in existence. According to Campbell (2010), while the number of women participating in intercollegiate athletics in 2003 was slightly over 200,000, the number of men participating in intercollegiate athletics was nearly 300,000. Therefore, as this evidence suggests, there is still a need for the enforcement of Title IX.

As a means of determining compliance with Title IX, the Office of Civil Rights developed three prongs (Causby, 2010). According to Staurowsky (2009), to be in compliance with Title IX, schools must meet at least one of the following three prongs:

1. Participation opportunities for male and female students are provided in numbers substantially proportionate to their respective enrollments.
2. The school can show a history and continuing practice of program expansion that is demonstrably responsive to the developing interest and abilities of the members of that sex.
3. The school can demonstrate that the present program fully and effectively accommodates the interests and abilities of the members of that sex. (p. 57)

According to Almond and Cohen (2005), the Office of Civil Rights has referred to the three prongs as a safe harbor signifying to institutions that liability will be waived if they could satisfy at least one of the three prongs.

According to Burnett (2003), acquiring compliance through the SP prong, is the only true prong that is safe due to the statistical nature and apparent understanding of that prong. The requirements for the continued expansion and full accommodation prongs are intrinsically too broad and do not have clear cut objectives to make a legal, justifiable argument for compliance (Almond & Cohen, 2005). Consequently, the most common method of measuring compliance with Title IX accepted by the court of law is the SP prong (Pelek, 2008), and according to Stafford (2004), by default has become the primary standard to measure Title IX compliance. Although the Office of Civil Rights has never directly defined SP, in practice, it is achieved when the percentage of female athletes at an institution is within five percentage points of the percentage of full-time females enrolled at the institution (Anderson & Cheslock, 2004). However, in discussing Title IX issues in athletic programs at collegiate institutions, Lamber (2000) argued that the proportionality prong's best feature is also its most significant disadvantage and is controversial for numerous reasons.

According to Lamber (2000), most opponents of Title IX attack the statute as a quota while other opponents argue that participation rates speak to only one aspect of compliance with Title IX without taking into account how an institution is complying in other parts of the legislation. Moreover, the opponents argue that such quotas harm athletic opportunities for males. Nevertheless, according to Lamber, even with these criticisms of the SP prong it still represents the best measure of Title IX compliance because of the even greater challenges presented by the other prongs.

The second prong of Title IX compliance is for the school to demonstrate a history and continuing practice of expanding opportunities for the underrepresented gender (Stafford, 2004). However, according to Stafford, the steps to demonstrate a history and continuing practice of expanding opportunities at institutions are unclear. However, the courts have determine that adding more student athletes to existing women's teams is not the correct path to address increasing participation rates for women (Rosner & Shropshire, 2004). Furthermore, the courts have not found that any institution has satisfied the continued expansion prong of Title IX compliance (Stafford, 2004).

The third prong of Title IX compliance is to show full accommodation of the interest and abilities of the underrepresented sex (Stafford, 2004). Full accommodation means the institutions have met all the athletic interests of the underrepresented gender (Mumford, 2006). Exactly like the second prong of continued expansion, no institution has been able to satisfy the prong of full accommodation or even provide adequate proof of it in the courts (Stafford, 2004). Thus, SP is in practice the best avenue to address the conditions for Title IX compliance (Carpenter & Acosta, 2005). Nevertheless, even with the SP prong, Title IX compliance is an on-going challenge in the fight to achieve gender equity in intercollegiate athletics (Schneider et al., 2010).

In an effort to achieve and monitor Title IX compliance, the United States Congress passed the Equity in Athletic Disclosure Act (EADA) in 1994 (DeHass, 2008). The EADA required all coeducational institutions of higher education that participated in the federal student financial aid program and sponsored intercollegiate athletic programs to provide, on an annual basis, specific information regarding their athletic programs to the Office of Civil Rights. Also as a result of the EADA, the Office of Postsecondary Education created the Equity in Athletics Data Analysis Cutting Tool website, which recorded institutions' responses to the EADA Survey and is available to the public (DeHass, 2008).

## Empirical Evidence and Title IX

This section of the literature review discusses empirical studies related to Title IX compliance. Empirical evidence related to Title IX compliance identified in the literature was either direct measures of Title IX compliance or perceptions of Title IX compliance. Consequently, of this portion of the literature review is organized by measures of compliance and perceptions of compliance.

### Examination of Title IX Compliance

A study conducted by Beam et al. (2004) offered but one example of the importance of Title IX compliance. According to Beam et al., the passage of Assembly Bill 2295 by the California legislature in 2002 required that the California Department of Education and the California Postsecondary Commission contract with an independent evaluator to study Title IX compliance in the high schools, community colleges and universities in the state. Subsequently, Beam and associates were contracted to complete the study.

In conducting the study, Beam et al. (2004) utilized the following three data sources: (a) surveys distributed to a representative sample of high schools, and all of the community colleges and universities in California, (b) online EADA Survey data, and (c) site visits to select high schools, community colleges, and universities. Of particular interest to the current study are the findings related to the postsecondary institutions.

The participants for the postsecondary segment of the study conducted by Beam et al. (2004) included the athletic directors of 28 universities and 89 community collegesin the state of California. The results of the analysis of data used to determine SP revealed that many of the postsecondary institutions in the state were not in compliance with the SP prong of Title IX. At the university level, only 57% of the responding universities were in compliance with the SP prong of Title IX. Another significant finding was the difference between the perceptions of the athletic directors regarding Title IX compliance and actual figures documented in the EADA Survey. According to survey data that measured athletic directors' perceptions, 25 of the 28 university athletic directors indicated that their school had female athletic participation rates within 5% of enrollment. However, EADA Survey data indicated that only 16 of the 28 universities met the SP prong of Title IX. The other 12 universities had discrepancies between enrollment and athletic participation ranging from 6% to over 10%.

Although Beam et al. (2004) found that 43% of the universities did not meet the SP prong, the authors found that the universities were clearly doing a better job with Title IX compliance than the community colleges. At the community college level, the percentage of institutions that met the SP prong was drastically lower. At the community college level, only 8% of the responding community colleges met the SP prong. The authors found that while females accounted for 54% of the full-time student enrollment at the community colleges, they only represented 35% of the athletic population. These figures resulted in a gap of 19% rather than the less than 5% gap required by the SP prong. When participation rates were examined by community college, the authors found that of the 89 responding institutions, 87 had a smaller percentage of female athletes than the percentage of full-time female students. Moreover, according to Beam et al., 84% of the responding community colleges had discrepancies between female enrollment and female athletic participation that exceeded 10%.

A study conducted by Anderson and Cheslock (2004) used EADA Survey data to examine Title IX compliance. The authors used data from the 1995-96 and 2001-02 academic years to examine SP compliance and strategies used to achieve SP compliance. Specifically, Anderson and Cheslock examined evidence to determined if schools were achieving compliance by actually increasing opportunities for females to participate in athletics, or if they were merely decreasing the opportunities afforded to male athletes. According to the authors, part of the significance of their study was that unlike most studies that only examined Division I institutions, their study included institutions form Divisions I, II, and III.

To answer their research question, the authors first compared athleticparticipation rates and enrollment rates of the 1995-1996 school year to the athletic participation rates and the enrollment rates of the 2001-2002 school year for 703 National Collegiate Athletic Association (NCCA) institutions. Using EADA Survey data, the authors found that between the years of 1995-96 and 2001-02 the percentage of schools that met the SP prong increased from about 7 to 10% in the 1995-96 year to about 11 to 18% in 2001-02 year. In which case, the authors noted that more institutions were meeting the SP prong of Title IX in 2002 than they were in 1996. Further analysis indicated that the increase was the result of an average increase of one women's sport and 27 female athletes and no increase in the number of men's sports offered and an average increase of only two male athletes. Consequently, the results of the study indicated that positive changes in gender equity were taking place and contrary to the question posed in the title of the article, *Does Title IX Harm Male Athletes?* (Anderson & Cheslock, 2004), the results of the study indicated that Title IX compliance did not harm male athletes when it increased opportunities for women.

Similar to the study conducted by Anderson and Cheslock (2004), Campbell's (2010) study examined not only measures of Title IX compliance but also factors that distinguished compliant institutions from noncompliant institutions. Using data retrieved from the EADA Survey, Campbell examined compliance measures of 258 National Association of Intercollegiate Athletics (NAIA) schools across the nation. The results of the author's analysis of data revealed that only 11% of the 258 NAIA schools met the SP prong of Title IX during the 2007 academic year. While the 258 schools had a full-time undergraduate student enrollment that was 58% female, the athletic participation rate for females was only 40%. Consequently, the aggregated data for the 258 NAIA schools resulted in an 18 percentage point discrepancy between female enrollment and female sports participation. The only distinguishing factor between compliant and noncompliant schools identified by Campbell was in the sports offered at the schools. Campbell found that schools with football programs were more likely to be noncompliant than schools without football programs.

Although there is evidence that Title IX has made an impact in terms of providing opportunities for females to participate in intercollegiate athletics, much of the evidence suggests that there is not equality in terms of gender. When EADA Survey data were examined, the vast majority of postsecondary institutions that offered athletic programs still did not meet the SP prong of Title IX. Consequently, there continues to be a need to monitor what institutions are doing to achieve or maintain compliance.

**Perceptions of Title IX Compliance**

A review of the literature revealed that in addition to researchers utilizing factual EADA Survey data to examine Title IX compliance other researchers have examined perceptions of Title IX compliance. This section of the literature discusses studies that have examined the perceptions of different populations of individuals concerning Title IX compliance.

One of the populations studied was that of women athletic administrators. To determine the extent to which Title IX compliance areas are addressed in NCAA women's athletic programs, Schneider et al. (2010) gathered the perceptions of Senior Women Athletic Administrators (SWA). SWA are amongst the highest ranking athletic department officials and are responsible for women's intercollegiate athletics programs at the institution. A survey developed by Schneider et al. was emailed to all 841 SWA of the NCAA. The authors had a 48% response rate (406 respondents). While not a requirement of the SWA position, nearly all (99.7%) of the respondents were female.

The results of the analysis of data collected revealed that the majority of SWA perceived that men's and women's sports programs were equally provided for in each of the 13 areas assessed in Title IX. However, 31% of the respondents did not agree that men's and women's sports received the same amount of publicity. Particularly noteworthy of this study was that there was not an area assessed on the survey where there was 100% agreement from the participating SWA. This indicates that even high level athletic administrators realize that there is room for improvement in terms of Title IX compliance. Table 2 provides the percentages of respondents who agreed and disagreed that there was gender equality in the 13 Title IX compliance areas at their institutions.

Table 2

Perceptions of Senior Women Athletic Administrators Regarding Specific Areas of Title IX Compliance

| There is Gender Equality in: | Percentages of Strongly Disagree or Disagree | Percentages of Strongly Agree or Agree | Percentages of Neutral Responses |
|---|---|---|---|
| Publicity | 31.0% | 55.3% | 13.8% |
| Locker Room Facilities | 27.1% | 63.2% | 9.7% |
| Coaching | 20.0% | 70.2% | 9.7% |
| Recruitment of Student Athletes | 15.4% | 73.2% | 11.4% |
| Tutoring | 6.3% | 74.3% | 19.4%% |
| Support Services | 10.3% | 76.0% | 13.7% |
| Equipment & Supplies | 17.7% | 77.7% | 7.6% |
| Competitive Facilities | 10.8% | 78.4% | 10.8% |
| Practice Facilities | 10.6% | 78.7% | 10.8% |
| Travel & Per Diem Allowances | 12.2% | 80.5% | 7.4% |
| Scheduling of Games | 10.7% | 81.1% | 8.1% |
| Medical & Training Facilities | 8.6% | 84.3% | 7.2% |
| Housing & Dining Facilities | 6.7% | 84.4 | 9.0% |

Mumford (1998) is one of the few researchers who examined perceptions of Title IX compliance in the community college population. Mumford sought to determine the perceptions of Title IX Compliance of the 18 athletic directors of the Maryland Junior College Athletic Conference (MJCAC). Of the 18 athletic directors in the MJCAC, 15 responded to the survey for an 83% response rate. In addition to the data gathered from the surveys, Mumford conducted interviews with six of the responding athletic directors.

Mumford's (1998) survey used a Likert scale with responses ranging from always to non-existent to determine the athletic directors' perceptions of Title IX compliance. Data gathered from the 15 returned surveys indicated that the majority (8) of the athletic directors perceived that their institution complied with the Title IX legislation. The remaining athletic directors (7) perceived that either their institutions were in compliance for the most part (5 athletic directors) or not all in compliance (2 athletic directors). When asked who is responsible for policy making decisions regarding equity, 73% (11)of the athletic directors perceived that athletic directors were one of the policy decision makers. Because of the findings of his study, Mumford recommended that the MJCAC officials provide professional development with regard to Title IX compliance to all member institutions and for the institutions to implement a comprehensive self-reviewed process with regards to gender equity.

Taken together, these findings suggest that while athletic directors have authority to make decisions regarding gender equity, their decisions did not always result in equitable athletic programs for men and women. However, Mumford (1998) failed to make this connection. Another limitation of Mumford's study is that only measures of athletic directors' perceptions were measured. The study would have provided more useful information if data from the EADA Survey had been included. The inclusion of EADA Survey data would have allowed Mumford to determine the accuracy of the athletic directors' perceptions of compliance by comparing their perceptions to the actual quantifiable data recorded on the survey. However, Mumford's study is significant because according to one of the items on the survey, over half (60%) of the participating athletic directors indicated that their institution had never conducted a gender equity self-study to determine the compliance with Title IX. Although Mumford's study was published nearly 15 years ago, a review of the literature did not reveal any other studies that examined whether or not institutions had conducted a gender equity self-study. Considering the importance of federal funding in most educational institutions, it would seem that not only would athletic directors but also institutions' presidents, would continually examine issues of gender equity rather than risk losing federal funding.

Unlike other studies that examined the perceptions of employees of public institutions with athletic programs, Parente (2008) examined the perceptions of student athletes. Parente emailed surveys to over 1,800 student-athletes attending Division III schools in the Allegheny Mountain College Conference (AMCC) to determine the perceptions of gender equity in intercollegiate sports. Of the 1,800 surveys distributed, 450 student athletes returned useable surveys for a response rate of 24%. The results of the analysis of data gathered revealed that 30% of the respondents believed that, in general, male athletes were treated better than female athletes. When only considering equipment and supplies provided by athletic departments, 46% of the respondents felt that men athletes received more and better supplies and equipment than women athletes. Consequently, many student athletes perceived the programs to be unequal.

A qualitative study conducted by Paule (2004) examined the perceptions of Title IX compliance from a broader perspective than the other researchers included in this review. Using interviews, Paule reported perceptions of an administrator, coaches, athletes, former athletes and students for a total sample size of 13. Although the information gathered from these individuals is not considered representative of the larger population of similar individuals, the results of the study provides valuable information regarding people's perceptions of the consequences of Title IX. The participants believed that Title IX has impacted women in a positive way; however they questioned whether the elimination of men's teams was justified.

Similar to the studies of Mumford (1998), Parente (2008), and Schneider et al. (2010); Causby (2010), examined the perceptions of athletic directors of two-year colleges that were members of either the NJCAA or the California Community College Athletic Association (CCCAA). Of the 624 member institutions, only 191 athletic directors responded to an online survey developed by Causby, resulting in an overall response rate of 32%. The respondents included 33 (17%) female athletic directors and 158 (83%) male athletic directors. While 95% of the respondents agreed that male and female athletes were provided the same opportunities and treatment across all sports, only 63% of the respondents indicated that their female athletic participation rates were within five percentage points of the overall female school enrollment. Therefore, according to survey responses, 37% of the athletic directors perceived that their schools had not met the SP prongs. However, when asked specifically if their schools were in compliance with Title IX, 74% of the athletic directors responded that their schools were in compliance. Maybe the most meaningful finding of Causby's study was that 91% of the respondents agreed that promotion of gender equity was a priority for their respective institutions. A limitation of Causby's study is that the author failed to include an analysis of data recorded in the EADA data tool. Analyzing the actual date recorded by the institutions in the EADA data tool would have provided a more objective snapshot of the institutions' Title IX compliance.

## Summary of Literature Review

The review of literature included a brief overview of the Mississippi public community and junior college and their development over time. The role of Title IX was also discussed with emphasis placed on introducing standards and procedures addressing compliance within intercollegiate athletics. Related literature was also presented that focused on findings addressing intercollegiate athletic participation related to compliance to Title IX compliance. The review concluded with findings addressing the overall perception of Title IX at institutions of higher learning from athletic directors, the students, and the institution. Strengths and weaknesses of the process were discussedalong with opportunities for improvement.

# CHAPTER III

# METHODOLOGY

Four research questions were designed to determine the perceptions of the athletic directors of the Mississippi's public community and junior colleges regarding Title IX compliance and their respective institution's compliance with the SP prong of Title IX. This chapter presents the methodology that was used to answer those research questions. This chapter is divided into the following major sections: research design, participants, instruments, procedure, and data analysis. This chapter concludes with a summary.

## Research Design

This study utilized a descriptive research design. Descriptive research, often used to determine attitudes, perceptions, and opinions, gathers numerical data to describe the current status of some phenomena (Airasian, Gay, & Mills, 2006). Descriptive research is often referred to as survey research because surveys are often used to collect data from the participants of the study. There are two types of descriptive studies that use surveys. A longitudinal survey collects data at least twice from either the same population or sample or different populations or samples (Airasian et al., 2006). Cross-sectional surveys, the other type of descriptive method, gather data from a selected group only once. This study used a cross-sectional descriptive method. The cross-sectional descriptive method was the most appropriate method to use to answer the research questions of this study. This method of research using the descriptive method of research facilitated discovering the perceptions of athletic directors of Mississippi's public community and junior colleges and to determine if the public community and junior colleges in Mississippi were in compliance with the SP prong of Title IX.

## Participants

Data for this study was gathered from the eight athletic directors and from the online EADA survey results of the 15 public community and junior colleges in the state of Mississippi. Therefore, in describing participants, it is appropriate to describe both the athletic directors of the 15 public community and junior colleges and the institutions they serve. Mississippi has 14 public community colleges and one junior college (Jones County Junior College). Full-time student enrollment at these institutions ranged from 1,572 (Southwest Mississippi Community College) to 9,820 (Hinds Community College). Table 1 in Chapter II displayed each of these institutions. All 15 of the institutions have intercollegiate athletic programs and they all receive federal funding from the U.S. Department of Education. Institution level data were gathered from the online EADA survey; therefore all 15 institutions are included in the analysis of data used to determine substantial proportionality for Title IX compliance.

Each institution has an athletic director who is responsible for overseeing the administration of the institution's athletic program. While all 15 of the athletic directors were invited to participate in the study, only 8 returned the Two Year Institution Title IX Survey. Of the 8 athletic directors who returned the survey, 7 were men and 1 was a woman.

## Instruments

Two instruments were used to gather data for this study. The first instrument, Two Year Institution Title IX Survey, was used to determine the perceptions of the athletic directors. The second instrument, EADA Survey was used to determine if the 15 community and junior colleges in the state of Mississippi are in compliance with the SP prong of Title IX. This section of the methodology describes both of those instruments.

### Two Year Institution Title IX Survey

The first instrument, Two Year Institution Title IX Survey, was used a modified version of the survey developed and used by Causby (2010); permission was given by Causby to use the survey (see Appendix A). Causby's survey was modified by deleting the items that were publically available online in the EADA survey portal as a means of decreasing the time required of the athletic directors to complete the survey.

The survey consisted of four sections. The first section of the survey was used to gather demographic data of the athletic directors and the institutions they serve. This section of the survey contained six closed-ended items.

The second section of the survey contained 12 closed-ended items designed to measure the athletic directors' perceptions of their institution's level of Title IX's compliance. The item choices for this section of the survey consisted of (a) Yes, (b) No, and (c) I Don't Know.

The third section of the survey consisted of 14 Likert scale items for a total of 14 items. The four-point Likert scale used in this section ranged from Not Effective (1) to Very Effective (4). The third section of the survey was designed to determine the athletic directors' perceptions of the effectiveness of specific strategies to maintain or achieve Title IX compliance.

The final section of the survey contained 19 closed-ended items. The Likert scale items were set on a four-point scale ranging from Strongly Disagree (1) to Strongly Agree (4).

The entire survey was online and contained 51 items with the vast majority of the items being close-ended. The survey can be completed in approximately 20 minutes. A copy of the online survey is available in the appendix (Appendix B).

**validity and reliability.** The validity and reliability of the Two Year Institution Title IX Survey was established by Causby (2010). According to Causby, a four-stage testing process was used to establish the validity and reliability of the instrument. The first two stages established content validity for the instrument. For stage 1, an initial draft of the survey was submitted for review by a panel of experts to evaluate the appropriateness of content, to test for significance it would be for community college athletic administrators, and to assess the extent to which the instrument measured what it was intended to measure. The panel of experts was comprised of four individuals with experience as athletic administrators at community colleges. After obtaining survey responses and feedback from the panel of experts, the instrument was evaluated and modified accordingly by Causby. Stage 2 incorporated an observation and think aloud protocol where an additional expert was asked to respond to the modified survey while in the presence of the researcher, who then made observations and recorded comments as the survey was completed. This process helped to evaluate cognitive and motivational aspects of the survey and ensured interpretation consistency, logical sequencing, and an overall positive survey presentation.

Stage 3 consisted of an online pilot test of the survey designed to emulate all the procedures proposed in Causby's (2010) study. According to Causby, this stage was used to assess the overall reliability of the instrument and to determine if instrument functioned as intended. A convenience sampling method was used to test the instrument among 20 community college athletic administrators that were not a part of his study sample. Pilot test participants were asked to complete the survey and to respond to key questions about the instrument including whether the instructions were clear and easily understandable and whether there were any particular items that were unclear or confusing. After completion of pilot testing, stage 4 consisted of a final review of the instrument by individuals who were not familiar with the content of the study. This final review was intended to identify any grammatical and/or formatting errors that were present. Consequently, Causby provided ample evidence to support the validity and reliability of the instrument. Although the instrument was modified for use in the current study, the modifications that were made did not compromise the validity and reliability that was established by Causby. The only modifications made were the elimination of items that collected institutional data that is publically available online. This modification was made to decrease the burden of the participants in completing the survey. In addition to the evidence provided by Causby and prior to use in the current study, the instrument was examined by this researcher and this researcher's dissertation advisor.

**EADA Survey**

The second instrument that was used in this study was the EADA Survey. The EADA survey was developed by the United States Department of Education (USDE, 2010) to document and track institutional commitment to Title IX compliance. Coeducational postsecondary institutions that participate in the federal student financial assistance program and that have intercollegiate athletic programsare required by section 485(g) of the Higher Education Act of 1965, as amended, 20 U.S.C. 1092 to complete the annual EADA survey (USDE, 2010). Moreover, the data collected with this survey are publically available on the Office of Postsecondary Education's Equity in Athletics Data Analysis Cutting Tool website.

The survey is organized into five categories. The first category collects screening items. These items are used to determine appropriate items for the remainder of the survey. The second category of items collects data related to athletics participation by sport and gender. The third category of the survey collects data related to coaching staff and salaries and the fourth category collects data related to revenues and expenses. The final category of the survey collects supplemental data. This section of the survey allows the respondent to include any information that he or she feels will help the reader understand all other aspects of the data. Respondents to the survey must record numerical data that describes their institution for all of the items on the survey. The estimated time to complete the survey is 5.5 hours.

Institutions are required by law to complete the survey by a certain time each year. However, the most recent data available for this study was the data collected in the 2010-2011 academic year. In which case, it appears that information is made public two years after the survey has been completed. There is no information recorded that explains the validity and reliability of the instrument.

## Procedures

Prior to data collection, approval to conduct the study was secured from the Institutional Review Board (IRB) at Mississippi State University (see Appendix C). Upon IRB approval, the researcher e-mailed the 15 athletic directors of the community and junior colleges in the state of Mississippi informing them of the study and asking them to participate. An informed consent document and a link to the online Two Year Institution Title IX Survey were also included in that e-mail. After the first deadline to complete the survey had passed, athletic directors who had not completed the survey were e-mailed again to ask for their participation by a certain time. After that time had elapsed, data were gathered from the online survey site and down loaded into a Statistical Package for Social Science (SPSS) program file. To determine SP Title IX compliance, data were exported from the Equity in Athletics Data Analysis Cutting Tool website to a SPSS data file.

## Data Analysis

The following research questions guided the study.

1. What are the perceptions of the athletic directors of Mississippi's public community and junior colleges regarding their institution's level of Title IX compliance? To answer this question, responses to items 1-12 on the second section of the Two Year Institution Title IX Survey were analyzed. Data were

analyzed using descriptive statistics. Specifically, frequencies and percentages were used to answer the research question.

2. What are the perceptions of the athletic directors of Mississippi's public community and junior colleges regarding the effectiveness of specific strategies to strengthen Title IX compliance efforts at their respective institutions? To answer this question, responses to item 1-14, which listed 14 strategies to achieve or maintain Title IX compliance, on the third section of the Two Year Institution Title IX Survey were analyzed. Data were analyzed using descriptive statistics. Specifically, means, modes, frequencies, and percentages were used to answer the research question.

3. What are the perceptions of the athletic directors of Mississippi's public community and junior colleges regarding barriers to Title IX compliance at their respective institutions? To answer this question, responses to items 1-19, which listed 19 barriers to achieving or maintaining Title IX compliance, on the fourth section of the Two Year Institution Title IX Survey were analyzed. Data were analyzed using descriptive statistics. Specifically, means, modes, frequencies, and percentages were used to answer the research question.

4. Are the public community and junior colleges in the state of Mississippi in compliance with the SP prong of Title IX? To answer this question, responses from the EADA survey were analyzed. To determine if the athletic participation of females was proportional to their full-time enrollment, percentages were calculated for enrollment (percentage of full-time enrollment represented by females) and athletic participation (percentage of total athletic population

represented by females). To be in compliance with Title IX, the difference between the two should not exceed 5%.

Data collected from both surveys were entered into SPSS for analysis. All data used to answer the research questions were analyzed using descriptive statistics. Specifically, frequencies, percentages, modes, and means were calculated to answer the research questions.

**Summary**

Chapter III discussed the methodology that was used to fulfill the purpose of the study. The purpose of this study was to determine the perceptions of the athletic directors of the 15 public community and junior colleges in the state of Mississippi regarding Title IX compliance and to determine if their respective institutions were in compliance with the SP prong of Title IX. To fulfill this purpose, a descriptive research design was used. Data was gathered by the use of two surveys. One of the surveys was a modified version of the survey first used by Causby (2010). The second survey, EADA Survey, was the mandatory survey required by the United States Department of Education for all public co-educational institutions with intercollegiate athletic programs that receive federal funds. Eight of the 15 athletic directors completed the Two Year Institution Title IX Survey and data were collected for all 15 institutions from the EADA Survey. All data collected were transferred to a SPSS data file which was used to compute descriptive statistics to answer the research questions.

# CHAPTER IV

# RESULTS

The purpose of this study was to determine the perceptions of the athletic directors of the 15 public community and junior colleges in Mississippi regarding Title IX compliance and to determine if their respective institutions are in compliance with the SP prong of Title IX. To fulfill the purpose of this study, four research questions were developed. Chapter IV presents the results of the analysis of data that were used to answer each research question and is organized by research question. The chapter will conclude with a summary of findings.

## Demographics

In July 2009, the online Two Year Title IX Survey was distributed through email to the athletic directors at the 15 public community and junior colleges in Mississippi. The overall response rate for the survey was 53% (8 of 15 athletic directors responded). However, for the athletic directors that did not respond to the survey, the researcher perceives that the athletic directors would have responded to the survey similar to the respondents. Of the 8 athletic directors who returned the survey, 87.5% (7) were men and 12.5% (1) was a woman. When examining experience, 62.5% (5) of the athletic directors have been working at their current institution and at the two-year level for 11 or more years. All 8 of the athletic directors indicated that their institutions have been participating in intercollegiate athletics for more than 40 years. Of the 3 prongs to Title IX compliance, the athletic directors indicated that their institution was using SP prong (12.5%), full accommodation (25%), and continued expansion (62.5%). Most importantly, all of the athletic directors indicated that the president at their institution had a very active and involved role in supporting athletic.

**Research Question 1**

Research question 1 asked: What are the perceptions of the athletic directors of Mississippi's public community and junior colleges regarding their institution's level of Title IX compliance? To answer this question, responses to items 1-12 on the second section of the Two Year Institution Title IX Survey were analyzed. Results are presented in Table 3.

For all of the items in this section of the survey except for item 1, seven athletic directors responded. For item 1, only six directors responded. Only two items (Items 2 and 7) on this section of the survey had total agreement among the seven responding athletic directors. All of the athletic directors indicated that the promotion of gender equity was a priority for their institution and that their respective institutions fully accommodated the interest and abilities of their students. However, only five of the seven athletic directors indicated that their institution was in compliance with Title IX. One athletic director indicated that his or her institution was not in compliance as the other one did not know whether or not their institution was in compliance. Nevertheless, for 10 of the 12 items, the majority of respondents indicated that their institutions were complying with Title IX legislation. The only two items that less than 50% of the respondents recorded a Yes answer were items 4 (A gender equity committee has been formed) and 9 (The institution belongs to a conference that has a plan for compliance to Title IX).

Only two of the athletic directors indicated that their institutions had a gender equity committee. The other five indicated that institution did not (3 athletic directors) or that they did not know if there was a gender equity committee (2 athletic directors). For item 9, the majority (57%) of responding athletic directors did not know if the conference that their institution belonged to had a plan for Title IX compliance. Also, noteworthy, is the finding that of the 12 items on this section of the survey, nine items had responses that at least one athletic director indicated that they did not know the answer. The only items that did not have an I Don't Know answer were items 2 (Add a varsity head coach to alleviate current coaching staff overload), 7 (Emphasize growth of participation by women in sports with large participation potential), and 10 (Limit squad sizes in sports for men). However, for the one item on this section of the survey that exemplifies the intent of Title IX, equal athletic opportunities for males and females, 86% of the athletic directors recorded a Yes response. Seven athletic directors indicated that their institutions provided males and female the same opportunities and treatment across all areas of the athletic program. Therefore, to answer Research Question 1, it appears that the majority of responding athletic directors of the public community and junior colleges in the state of Mississippi perceive that their institutions are complying with the Title IX legislation.

Table 3

Perceptions of Title IX Compliance Results

| Item | Item Statement | Frequency (Percentage) of each Response | | | n |
|---|---|---|---|---|---|
| | | Yes | No | I Don't Know | |
| 1 | A gender appropriate language policy is in place. | 4(66%) | 1(17%) | 1(17)% | 6 |
| 2 | The promotion of gender equity is a priority of the institution. | 7(100%) | 0(0%) | 0(0%) | 7 |
| 3 | All athletic staff are familiar with and understand theirresponsibilities regarding Title IX compliance. | 6(86%) | 0(0%) | 1(14%) | 7 |
| 4 | A gender equity committee has been formed. | 2(29%) | 3(42%) | 2(29%) | 7 |
| 5 | The sports interests of the student body have beenformally evaluated. | 4(57%) | 2(29%) | 1(14%) | 7 |
| 6 | A history and continuing practice of programexpansionresponsive to developing interests andabilities of members of the underrepresentedgender exists. | 5(71%) | 0(0%) | 2(29%) | 7 |
| 7 | Current sports offerings fully accommodate the interests and abilities of the institutions students. | 7(100%) | 0(0%) | 0(0%) | 7 |
| 8 | A plan to insure compliance or bring the institution into compliance with Title IX is in place. | 6(86%) | 0(0%) | 1(14%) | 7 |
| 9 | The institution belongs to a conference that has a plan for compliance to Title IX. | 3(43%) | 0(0%) | 4(57%) | 7 |
| 10 | Male and Female athletes are provided the same opportunities and treatment across all areas of the athletic program. | 6(86%) | 1(14%) | 0(0%) | 7 |
| 11 | The athletic program at my institution is in compliance with Title IX of the Education Amendments Act of 1972. | 5(71%) | 1(14.5%) | 1(14.5%) | 7 |
| 12 | Athletic participation opportunities for students are proportionate to overall female and male enrollments. | 4(57%) | 1(14%) | 2(29%) | 7 |

## Research Question 2

Research Question 2 asked: What are the perceptions of the athletic directors of Mississippi's public community and junior colleges regarding the effectiveness of specific strategies to strengthen Title IX compliance efforts at their respective institutions? To answer this question, responses to items 1-14, which listed 14 strategies to achieve or maintain Title IX compliance, on the third section of the Two Year Institution Title IX Survey were analyzed. The item choices (corresponding value) for this section of the survey were: Not Effective (1), Somewhat Effective (2), Effective (3), and Very Effective (4). While the scale with these choices is considered ordinal data by item, the item scores were summed to obtain interval data, which could be analyzed to provide mean scores. Therefore, the descriptive analysis of data included both means and modes. Results are presented in Tables 4 and 5.

The number of athletic directors responding to the 14 items on this section of the survey was either four or five (see Table 4). The results of data analysis indicated that for each of the 14 strategies listed, the average score was less than 3, the value associated with a perception of effective. Half (7) of the strategies listed had average scores less than 2, indicating that on average, the athletic directors did not perceive that these strategies (Strategies 3, 6, 7, 9,10, 13, and 14) were even somewhat effective in strengthening Title IX compliance. The other half of the survey strategy items had scores between 2.0 and 2.5, indicating that for these seven of the strategies (Strategies 1, 2, 4, 5, 8, 11, and 12), the athletic directors perceived them to be somewhat effective in strengthening Title IX compliance. Consequently, the average scores for all 14 strategy items indicated that the athletic directors, on average, did not perceive them to be effective means of strengthening Title IX compliance.

When strategy items were examined by frequency (mode) of choice selection, the most frequently occurring response across the 14 items was 1, Not Effective. For eight of the strategies (Strategies 3, 6, 7, 9, 10, 11, 13, and 14) listed, most of the responding athletic directors indicated that the strategy was not effective in strengthening Title IX compliance at their institution. However, for 12 of the 14 strategies listed, at least one athletic director indicated that the strategy was effective or very effective in strengthening Title IX compliance. The only strategy that was perceived by any of the athletic directors as being very effective was item 4. For this item, one athletic director perceived that creating a full-time assistant coach for women to help the current staff would be a very effective strategy to strengthen Title IX compliance at his or her institution. At the other end of the Likert scale (Not Effective), all of the responding athletic directors (n = 4) for item 9 (Reduce number of sports available to men) indicated that that was not an effective means of achieving or maintaining Title IX compliance. Nonetheless, the answer to Research Question 2 (What are the perceptions of the athletic directors of Mississippi's public community and junior colleges regarding specific strategies to strengthen Title IX compliance efforts at their respective institutions?) is that the athletic directors did not perceive the listed strategies to be effective in strengthening Title IX compliance at their respective institutions. Table 4 displays the survey items and the number and percentage for each item choice. Table 5 displays the results of data analysis used to answer Research Question 2.

Table 4

Number and Percentage of Item Choice Selections

| Item | Strategy | Frequency (percentage) of Response | | | |
|---|---|---|---|---|---|
| | | Not Effective | Somewhat Effective | Effective | Very Effective |
| 1 | An in-depth evaluation of Title IX compliance within the athletic department. | 0(0%) | 3(60%) | 2(40%) | 0(0%) |
| 2 | Add an intercollegiate sport and its head coach position for women. | 1(25%) | 1(25%) | 2(50%) | 0(0%) |
| 3 | Add a varsity head coach to alleviate current coaching staff overload. | 3(60%) | 1(20%) | 1(20%) | 0(0%) |
| 4 | Create a full-time assistant coach position for women to assist the current coaching staff. | 1(20%) | 2(40%) | 1(20%) | 1(20%) |
| 5 | Redistribute existing athletic budget dollars. | 1(20%) | 3(60%) | 1(20%) | 0(0%) |
| 6 | Invest special funds into the budget of the under-financed sports to enhance the number and quality of opportunities. | 2(40%) | 2(40%) | 1(20%) | 0(0%) |
| 7 | Emphasize growth of participation by women in sports with large participation potential (e.g. swimming, soccer, track and field, and cross country). | 3(60%) | 1(20%) | 1(20%) | 0(0%) |
| 8 | Fund the development and implementation of a plan to control attrition on women's teams | 1(25%) | 2(50%) | 1(25%) | 0(0%) |
| 9 | Reduce the number of sports available to men. | 4(100%) | 0(0%) | 0(0%) | 0(0%) |
| 10 | Limit squad sizes in sports for men. | 4(80%) | 0(0%) | 1(20%) | 0(0%) |
| 11 | Encourage a conference-wide standard of compliance to Title IX. | 2(40%) | 1(20%) | 2(40%) | 0(0%) |
| 12 | Fund-outreach programs for women to encourage involvement in sport | 1(20%) | 3(60%) | 1(20%) | 0(0%) |

| | | | | | |
|---|---|---|---|---|---|
| | activity. | | | | |
| 13 | Encourage the filing of formal grievances in the areas of non-compliance to Title IX in the athletic programs with the Title IX officer on campus. | 3(60%) | 1(20%) | 1(20%) | 0(0%) |
| 14 | Encourage the filing of formal grievances in the areas of non-compliance to Title IX in the athletic programs with the Title IX officer on campus. | 3(60%) | 2(40%) | 0(0%) | 0(0%) |

Table 5

Strategies to Strengthen Title IX Compliance Results

| Item | Strategy | Mean | Mode | n |
|---|---|---|---|---|
| 1 | An in-depth evaluation of Title IX compliance within the athletic department. | 2.4 | 2 | 5 |
| 2 | Add an intercollegiate sport and its head coach position for women. | 2.5 | 3 | 4 |
| 3 | Add a varsity head coach to alleviate current coaching staff overload. | 1.6 | 1 | 5 |
| 4 | Create a full-time assistant coach position for women to assist the current coaching staff. | 2.4 | 2 | 5 |
| 5 | Redistribute existing athletic budget dollars. | 2.0 | 2 | 5 |
| 6 | Invest special funds into the budget of the under-financed sports to enhance the number and quality of opportunities. | 1.8 | 1, 2 | 5 |
| 7 | Emphasize growth of participation by women in sports with large participation potential (e.g. swimming, soccer, track and field, and cross country). | 1.6 | 1 | 5 |
| 8 | Fund the development and implementation of a plan to control attrition on women's teams | 2.0 | 2 | 4 |
| 9 | Reduce the number of sports available to men. | 1.0 | 1 | 4 |
| 10 | Limit squad sizes in sports for men. | 1.4 | 1 | 5 |
| 11 | Encourage a conference-wide standard of compliance to Title IX. | 2.0 | 1, 3 | 5 |
| 12 | Fund-outreach programs for women to encourage involvement in sport activity. | 2.0 | 2 | 5 |
| 13 | Encourage the filing of formal grievances in the areas of non-compliance to Title IX in the athletic programs with the Title IX officer on campus. | 1.6 | 1 | 5 |
| 14 | Encourage the filing of formal grievances in the areas of | 1.4 | 1 | 5 |

| non-compliance to Title IX in the athletic programs with the Title IX officer on campus. | |

## Research Question 3

Research Question 3 asked: What are the perceptions of the athletic directors of Mississippi's public community and junior colleges regarding barriers to Title IX compliance at their respective institutions? To answer this question, responses to items 1-19 on the fourth section of the Two Year Institution Title IX Survey were analyzed. The Likert scale used for this section of the survey had item choices (corresponding values)of: Strongly Disagree (1), Disagree (2), Agree (3), and Strongly Agree (4). While the scale with these choices is considered ordinal data by item, the item scores were summed to obtain interval data, which could be analyzed to provide mean scores. Therefore, the descriptive analysis of data included both means and modes. Results are presented in Tables 6 and 7.

The 19 items consisted of selected barriers to Title IX compliance. Out of the 19 barriers listed, only one item (Barrier 6) had an average score that indicated that the athletic directors agreed was a barrier to Title IX compliance for their institutions. For this item, all five athletic directors either strongly agreed (two athletic directors) or agreed (three athletic directors) that lack of student interest in athletics because of other life priorities was a barrier to Title IX compliance for their institutions. There were only two other barriers listed where at least 50% of the responding athletic directors agreed that the barrier was relevant to their institutions. Two of the four athletic directors who responded to Barrier 7 (Lack of community/region support for female athletic programs) agreed with the statement. Consequently, it appears that the athletic directors perceived that of the listed barriers, the only barriers relevant to their institutions were related to lack of interest of females to participate in athletics and lack of community or region support for female athletics.

The average score for 18 of the 19 items on this section of the survey was less than 3, indicating that the majority of the barriers listed were not perceived by the athletic directors as barriers that affected their institutions' Title IX compliance. In fact, for nine of the 19 listed barriers, all of the participating athletic directors either strongly disagreed or disagreed that the barriers were in fact a barrier to their institutions Title IX compliance. The overall average for this section of the survey was 1.8, indicating an overall perception of strong disagreement with the survey barrier items. Consequently, the answer to Research Question 3 (What are the perceptions of the athletic directors of Mississippi's public community and junior colleges regarding barriers to Title IX compliance at their respective institutions?), is that the athletic directors did not perceive the listed barriers as barriers for the institutions in achieving or maintaining Title IX compliance. Table 6 displays the number and percentage for each choice selected by the participants and Table 7 displays the results of data analyzed to answer Research Question 3.

Table 6

Number and Percentage of Item Choice Selections

| Item | Barrier | Frequency (percentage) of Response | | | |
|---|---|---|---|---|---|
| | | Strongly Disagree | Disagree | Agree | Strongly Agree |
| 1 | The attitude of administrative superiors limits growth of athletics opportunities for women. | 4(80%) | 1(20%) | 0(0%) | 0(0%) |
| 2 | The attitude of administrative superiors that there are not equal numbers across gender of skilled athletes to participate in inter-collegiate sports. | 2(40%) | 3(60%) | 0(0%) | 0(0%) |
| 3 | Insufficient numbers of women in athletic leadership positions. | 1(20%) | 3(60%) | 1(20%) | 0(0%) |
| 4 | Insufficient numbers of female coaches in athletic department. | 1(20%) | 4(80%) | 0(0%) | 0(0%) |
| 5 | Insufficient numbers of full-time coaching position for female sports. | 1(20%) | 2(40%) | 2(40%) | 0(0%) |
| 6 | Lack of student interest because of other life priorities. | 0(0%) | 0(0%) | 3(60%) | 2(40%) |
| 7 | Lack of community/region support for female athletic program. | 0(0%) | 2(50%) | 2(50%) | 0(0%) |
| 8 | Inability to attract women into current athletic programs. | 0(0%) | 4(100%) | 0(0%) | 0(0%) |
| 9 | Inability to retain women in athletic program. | 0(0%) | 4(80%) | 1(20%) | 0(0%) |

| Item | Barrier | Frequency (percentage) of Response | | | |
|---|---|---|---|---|---|
| | | Strongly Disagree | Disagree | Agree | Strongly Agree |
| 10 | A finite number of budget dollars causes a reaction to protect present budgets, thus limiting support for growth in programs for women. | 2(40%) | 3(60%) | 0(0%) | 0(0%) |
| 11 | A finite number of budget dollars causes a reaction to protect present budgets, thus limiting support for growth in programs for women. | 2(40%) | 3(60%) | 0(0%) | 0(0%) |
| 12 | External support and financial resources(booster club, fund raising). | 2(40%) | 2(40%) | 1(20%) | 0(0%) |
| 13 | Unequal facilities (locker rooms, offices, practice space). | 3(60%) | 2(40%) | 0(0%) | 0(0%) |
| 14 | Unequal/unavailable financial support to recruit female. | 3(60%) | 2(40%) | 0(0%) | 0(0%) |

Table 6 Continued

Number and Percentage of Item Choice Selections

| Item | Barrier | Frequency (percentage) of Response | | | |
|---|---|---|---|---|---|
| | | Strongly Disagree | Disagree | Agree | Strongly Agree |
| 15 | A socialization process in the United States which does not promote the participation of both genders in sport to the same extent | 2(40%) | 2(40%) | 1(20%) | 0(0%) |
| 16 | An overall lack of understanding of Title IX compliance regulations | 2(40%) | 2(40%) | 1(20%) | 0(0%) |
| 17 | Lack of centralized conference/association level training and compliance program available | 2(40%) | 2(40%) | 1(20%) | 0(0%) |
| 18 | Title IX regulations do not account for differences between two and four-year athletic program | 1(20%) | 3(60%) | 1(20%) | 0(0%) |
| 19 | Current Title IX's legislation is not effective in ensuring gender equity in intercollegiate athletics at the two-year college level | 1(20%) | 4(80%) | 0(0%) | 0(0%) |

Table 7

Barriers to Title IX Compliance Results

| Item | Barrier | Mean | Mode | n |
|---|---|---|---|---|
| 1 | The attitude of administrative superiors limits growth of athletics opportunities for women. | 1.2 | 1 | 5 |
| 2 | The attitude of administrative superiors that there are not equal numbers across gender of skilled athletes to participate in inter-collegiate sports. | 1.7 | 2 | 5 |
| 3 | Insufficient numbers of women in athletic leadership positions. | 2.0 | 2 | 5 |
| 4 | Insufficient numbers of female coaches in athletic department. | 1.8 | 2 | 5 |
| 5 | Insufficient numbers of full-time coaching position for female sports. | 2.2 | 2, 3 | 5 |
| 6 | Lack of student interest because of other life priorities. | 3.4 | 3 | 5 |
| 7 | Lack of community/region support for female athletic program. | 2.5 | 2, 3 | 4 |
| 8 | Inability to attract women into current athletic programs. | 2.0 | 2 | 4 |
| 9 | Inability to retain women in athletic program. | 2.2 | 2 | 5 |
| 10 | A finite number of budget dollars causes a reaction to protect present budgets, thus limiting support for | 1.6 | 2 | 5 |

|    |                                                                                                                                                | |      |   |
|----|------------------------------------------------------------------------------------------------------------------------------------------------|-----|------|---|
|    | growth in programs for women.                                                                                                                  |     |      |   |
| 11 | A finite number of budget dollars causes a reaction to protect present budgets, thus limiting support for growth in programs for women.        | 1.6 | 2    | 5 |
| 12 | External support and financial resources(booster club, fund rising).                                                                           | 1.8 | 1, 2 | 5 |
| 13 | Unequal facilities (locker rooms, offices, practice space).                                                                                    | 1.4 | 1    | 5 |
| 14 | Unequal/unavailable financial support to recruit female.                                                                                       | 1.4 | 1    | 5 |
| 15 | A socialization process in the United States which does not promote the participation of both genders in sport to the same extent.             | 1.8 | 1, 2 | 5 |
| 16 | An overall lack of understanding of Title IX compliance regulations.                                                                           | 1.8 | 1, 2 | 5 |
| 17 | Lack of centralized conference/association level training and compliance program available.                                                    | 1.8 | 1, 2 | 5 |
| 18 | Title IX regulations do not account for differences between two and four-year athletic program.                                                | 2.0 | 2    | 5 |
| 19 | Current Title IX's legislation is not effective in ensuring gender equity in intercollegiate athletics at the two-year college level.          | 1.8 | 2    | 5 |

**Research Question 4**

Research question 4 asked: Are the public community and junior colleges in the state of Mississippi in compliance with the SP prong of Title IX? To answer this question, responses recorded on the EADA survey were analyzed. The data analyzed to answer this research question is an accurate measure for all 15 public community and junior colleges in the state of Mississippi. To determine if the 15 public community and junior colleges were in compliance with the SP prong of Title IX, measures of full-time female enrollment and female athletic participation at each institution was gathered from the EADA Survey.

To determine if the athletic participation of females was proportional to their full-time enrollment, percentages were calculated for enrollment (percentage of full-time enrollment represented by females) and athletic participation (percentage of total athletic population represented by females). To be in compliance with Title IX, the difference between the two should not exceed 5%. The results of analysis to answer Research Question 4 indicated that none of the 15 public community and junior colleges in the state of Mississippi were in compliance with the SP prong of Title IX. Table 8 displays the proportionality of enrollment and athletic participation and the difference between the two. Table 8 also displays the difference between the 5% mandated by the SP prong of Title IX and the actual difference for each institution. As displayed in Table 8, each institution fails to meet SP by at least 15 percentage points. Consequently, the answer to Research Question 4 is no, the 15 public community and junior colleges in the state of Mississippi are not in compliance with the SP prong of Title IX.

Table 8

Title IX SP Compliance by Institution

| Institution | Full-Time Female Percentage of Enrollment | Female Percentage of Athletic Participation | Difference | In Excess of SP |
|---|---|---|---|---|
| Coahoma Community College | 63.3% | 20.7% | 42.6% | 37.6 |
| Copiah-Lincoln Community College | 63.9% | 29.8% | 34.1% | 29.1 |
| East Central Community College | 60.9% | 30.7% | 30.2% | 25.2 |
| East Mississippi Community College | 58.5% | 25.3% | 33.2% | 28.2 |
| Hinds Community College | 63.3% | 36% | 27.3% | 22.3 |
| Holmes Community College | 64.0% | 29.5% | 34.5% | 29.5 |

| | | | | |
|---|---|---|---|---|
| Itawamba Community College | 61.0% | 28% | 33.0% | 28.0 |
| Jones County Junior College | 59.1% | 31% | 28.1% | 23.1 |
| Meridian Community College | 66.5% | 46.1% | 20.4% | 15.4 |
| Mississippi Delta Community College | 62.4% | 25.7% | 36.7% | 31.7 |
| Mississippi Gulf Coast Community College | 59.8% | 27.1% | 32.7% | 27.7 |
| Northeast Mississippi Community College | 58.9% | 28.3% | 30.6% | 25.6 |
| Northwest Mississippi Community College | 61.9% | 28.5% | 33.4% | 28.4 |
| Pearl River Community College | 60.0% | 30.7% | 29.3% | 24.3 |
| Southwest Mississippi Community College | 58.7% | 26.4% | 32.3% | 27.3 |
| All 15 Institutions | 61.7% | 29.9% | 31.8% | 26.8 |

**Summary**

This chapter presented the results of data analysis used to answer the four research questions that guided this study. To answer Research Questions 1-3, data recorded on the Two year Institution Title IX Survey by the participating athletic directors were analyzed. The results of this analysis indicated that (a) the majority of responding athletic directors perceived that their institution was in compliance with Title IX, (b) the majority of responding athletic directors perceived that the vast majority of the listed strategies for Title IX compliance were not effective for their institutions, and (c) the majority of responding athletic directors perceived that of the listed barriers, the only barriers relevant to their institutions are related to lack of interest of females to participate in athletics and lack of community or region support for female athletics. The results of the analysis of data to determine if the community and junior colleges in Mississippi were in compliance with the SP prong of Title IX indicated that neither of the institutions were in compliance. In fact, they all exceeded the five percentage points mandated by the SP prong by at least 15 percentage points.

CHAPTER V

SUMMARY, DISCUSSION, AND RECOMMENDATIONS

Chapter V includes a summary of the study, discussion of the findings of the study, and recommendations based on those finding. The chapter begins with a summary of Chapters I-IV then discusses the findings of the study. The chapter concludes with recommendations for public community and junior college leaders and recommendations for further research.

**Summary**

In the United States, community colleges are important to providing educational opportunities; over 40% of all students enrolled in higher educational institutions are attending community colleges (AACC, 2012). According to Brawer and Cohen (2003) community colleges are the institutions of choice for many students to further their educational journey and in athletics. Furthermore, AACC (2012) stated that 57% of the 12 million students enrolled in community colleges are women.

However, the opportunities afforded men and women have not always been equitable in education or athletics according to Burgess (2005). Gender equality is essential to the success of institutions therefore Title IX was developed to address the tensions of equality for men and women. Title IX of the Education Amendments of 1972 stated that "No person in the United States shall, on the basis of sex, be excluded from participation in, be denied the benefits of, or be subjected to discrimination under any educational program or activity receiving federal financial assistance" (USDJ, 2001, p.

7). The primary issue that supports this study is gender equity in community college athletic programs. The purpose of this study was to determine the perceptions of the athletic directors of the 15 public community and junior colleges in Mississippi regarding Title IX compliance and to determine if their respective institutions are in compliance with the SP prong of Title IX. To fulfill the purpose of the study, four research questions were developed. Three of the questions addressed the perceptions of Title IX compliance of athletic directors and one of the questions addressed the Title IX SP prong compliance of the 15 public community and junior colleges in Mississippi.

Chapter II provided a review of the literature that informed the present study. Certain researchers checked the actually compliance of institution using the SP prong. Beam et al. (2004) using the SP prong to determine compliance, revealed that many of the postsecondary institutions in the state of California were not in compliance with the SP prong of Title IX. Anderson and Cheslock(2004) revealed that Title IX compliance did not harm male athletes when it increased opportunities for women. Similar to the previous studies, Campbell's (2010) study revealed that the vast majority of postsecondary institution that offer athletic programs still did not meet the SP prong of Title IX. Consequently, the studies revealed that there still a need to monitor what institutions are doing to comply with Title IX.

Chapter III presented the methodology that was used to fulfill the purpose of the study. To fulfill the purpose of this study, a descriptive research design was used. Data were gathered using two surveys. One of the surveys was a modified version of the survey first used by Causby (2010). The second survey, the EADA Survey, was the mandatory survey required by the United States Department of Education for all public coeducational institution with intercollegiate athletic programs that receive federal funds. Eight of the 15 athletic directors completed the Two Year Institution Title IX Survey and data was collected for all 15 institutions from the EADA Survey. All data collected were transported to a SPSS data file which was used to compute descriptive statistic to answer the research questions.

Chapter IV presented the results of the analysis of data that were used to answer the research questions. To answer research questions 1-3, data recorded on the Two year Institution Title IX Survey by the 8 participating athletic directors were analyzed. The results of this analysis indicated that (a) overall the athletic directors perceived their institutions to be in compliance with Title IX, (b) overall the athletic directors perceived their institutions needed an in-depth evaluation of Title IX would be the best strategy to addressing compliance, and (c) overall it appears the athletic directors perceived that of the listed barriers, the only barriers relevant to their institutions are related to lack of interest of females to participate in athletics and lack of community or region support for female athletics.

The answer for research question 4 was obtained by analyzing data recorded on the EADA survey completed by all 15 public community and junior colleges in the state of Mississippi. The results of this analysis indicated that none of the institutions were in compliance with Title IX using the SP prong. Consequently, the purpose of this study was fulfilled. The analysis of data resulted in answers to each of the four research questions that guided this study.

## Discussion

This section of Chapter V includes a discussion of the findings of this study and relates those findings to prior research. This section also includes discussion on how this study contributes to the gaps in the literature as well as the limitations of the study. Similar to the section on the findings of the study in chapter IV, the findings of the study are discussed by research questions.

Research question 1 examined the perception of the levels of compliance from athleticdirectors at Mississippi's public community and junior colleges regarding their perspective school's compliance with Title IX. The findings for research question 1 revealed athletic directors perceived that their institutions met that the requirements of Title IX using either substantial proportionality, full accommodation, and continued expansion. Also, the finding revealed that athletic directors in Mississippi's public community and junior colleges perceived that the athletic program at their institution is in compliance with Title IX of the Education Amendments Act of 1972.

The findings were consistent with the findings from the research study conducted by Causby (2010) which revealed that majority of the athletic directors of two-year colleges that were members of either the NJCAA or CCCAA perceived that their institutions were in compliance with Title IX. However, a small amount of the athletics director from Causby's study perceived that their institution did not comply with the SP prong for Title IX similar with the finding of the present study. The present study revealed that over half of the athletics perceived that their institution complied using the SP prong in which athletic participation opportunities for students are proportionate to overall female and male enrollments. The findings for research question 1 also indicated that majority of the athletic directors perceived that the promotion of gender equity is a priority at their institution. Also, majority of the athletic director perceived that a plan to insure compliance or bring the institution into compliance with Title IX is in place at their institution. The present findings were consistent with the findings of Mumford (1998) who found that data gathered from the surveys indicated that majority of the athletic directors perceived that their school complied with Title IX as it pertains to gender equity. Consequently, the findings revealed that the majority of the responding athletic directors perceived that their institutions complied with Title IX of the Education Amendments of 1972.

Research question 2 examined the perceptions of the athletic directors of Mississippi's public community and junior colleges regarding the effectiveness of specific strategies to strengthen Title IX compliance efforts at their respective institutions. The present study revealed the majority of the athletic directors perceived that limiting squad sizes in sports for men is not effective when attempting to comply with Title IX. Also, majority of the athletic directors perceived reducing the number of sports available to men is not effective as a strategy for institutions to comply with Title IX. Similar to findings from Paule (2004), the respondents perceived that the elimination of men's team not to be justified.

Anderson and Cheslock (2004) wanted to know if school were achieving compliance by actually increasing opportunities for females to participate in athletics or were they merely decreasing the opportunities afforded to males. The results of the study indicated that Title IX did not impact male athletes negatively but did increase opportunities for women. The present study had similar findings.

However the most effective strategy perceived by the athletic directors from the present study would be to have an in-depth evaluation of Title IX compliance within the athletic department. Also, funding outreach programs for women to encourage involvement in sport activity was perceive to be a top strategy to complying with Title IX by the athletic directors. Furthermore, the redistributing existing athletic budget dollars was an effective strategy to comply with Title IX according to the athletic directors. However, the findings of Mumford (1998) revealed that over half of the participating athletic directors indicated that their institution had never conducted a gender equity self-study to determine the compliance with Title IX. Therefore, the findings revealed for the most part, the majority of responding athletic directors did not perceive the listed strategies effective in strengthening Title IX compliance at their institution.

Research question 3 examined the perceptions of the athletic directors of Mississippi's public community and junior colleges barriers to Title IX compliance at their respective institution. The present study revealed that the athletic directors strongly disagreed or agreed that the current Title IX's legislation is not effective in ensuring gender equity in intercollegiate athletics at the two-year college level was not a barrier to Title IX. Furthermore, the athletic directors did not perceive that the attitude of administrative superiors limits growth of athletics opportunities for women was not a barrier to complying with Title IX. However, Causby (2010) found that the lack of understand of Title IX's legislation was a barrier to compliance of to the requirements of Title IX. Also, Causby (2010) revealed that the lack of student interest because of life priorities was the barrier that majority of the athletic directors perceived that hindered the institutions towards comply with Title IX. Similarly, the finding in the present studyrevealed that the major barrier to compliance was the lack of student interest because of other life priorities perceived by the athletic director. Consequently, it appears the athletic directors perceived that of the listed barriers, the only barriers relevant to their institutions are related to lack of interest of females to participate in athletics and lack of community or region support for female athletics. This finding suggests that the responding athletic directors may perceive that these two barriers are not within their focus of control.

Research question 4 examined the compliance of public community and junior colleges in the state of Mississippi using the SP prong of Title IX. The present study reveal that the athletic directors overall indicated that at their institution they either used substantial proportionality, full accommodation, or continued expansion to comply with Title IX. Only one institution used substantial proportionality to comply with Title IX. The majority of the institution used continued expansion to comply with Title IX for the present study. The findings were consistent with the findings from the research study conducted by Beam et al. (2004) revealed majority of community college athletic directors in California reported that they did not use the SP prong to comply with Title IX. The majority of the institutions indicated that their school had achieved compliance by continued expansion (Beam et al., 2004). Finding from both studies suggested that most institutions would prefer to use continued expansion as a means to comply with Title IX versus SP prong.

Beam et al. (2004) also found that the largest gaps in enrollment and athletic participation were in the community college sector in California. Furthermore, the authors found that the institutions were not in compliance with Title IX using the SP prong; the majority of the students at the institution were female, only a small amount of the athletes were women. The present study had similar finding that majority of the students that attend the public community and junior colleges in Mississippi were female. Female students participating in athletics were determined by the study not to be in compliance using the SP prong of Title IX. Both of the finding revealed that public community and junior colleges were struggling to comply with Title IX using the SP prong. Consequently, the researcher concluded that none of the institutions in Mississippi were in compliance with Title IX using the SP prong.

However, the research would suggest from examining full-time enrollment and athletic participation of students at public community and junior colleges in Mississippi that taking on-line courses maybe a factor in not reaching compliance with Title IX. Education has recently been offered in a different fashion, since the use of the internet has emerged some institutions have begun offering online courses in which gives students opportunities to take courses at home rather than going to campus (Mississippi Association of Community and Junior Colleges, 2007). Full-time enrollment may drop down for female students if online courses were not used in establishing a full-time student and the percentages of differences using the SP prong towards Title IX maybe closer than from the present study results. Consequently, the researcher concluded that taking on-line courses affects the SP prong towards Title IX compliance.

The research examined the feminist legal theory. The present study revealed that the athletic directors indicated the promotion of gender equity is a priority at their institution. Furthermore, the athletic director indicated that their institution had in place a plan to insure compliance or bring the institution into compliance with Title IX. The findings were consistent with the feminist legal theory which suggests that laws and institutions must be continually examined as understanding and knowledge increases to satisfy the goal of equality for women (Hunter, 2012). Also, Brake (2001) stated that in athletics, as in other areas of feminist concern, there is tension among feminist scholars about how best to respond to conditions of inequality and resulting difference in treatment between men and women in society. Similarly in the present study, the athletic directors indicated that the lack of student interest because of other life priorities is a barrier toward meeting equality for women. Consequently, the researcher concluded that the feminist legal theory plays an important role in law for institutions to continually to evaluate gender equality and increase the understanding toward complying with Title IX.

## Recommendations

The final section of this dissertation provides recommendations. As a result of the findings of this study, two distinct categories of recommendations are provided. The first categories of recommendations are recommendations for public community and junior college leaders and are thereby designated as institutional recommendations. The second category recommendations are related to research needs and are designated as research recommendations.

### Institutional Recommendations

With 37,774 female students out of a total student population of 61,180 attending Mississippi's public community and junior colleges full time, it is important for the leaders at these educational institutions to be knowledgeable and aware of issues pertaining to Title IX and gender equity. With a compliance gap of 38.1%, continued attention to achieving Title IX compliance is important to close the gap using substantial proportionality.

To fully examine the potential benefits of Title IX compliance, it is recommended from the findings that the leaders at these institutions implement an annual equity training program for athletic directors, coaches, and athletic staff to ensure their program would know how to comply with Title IX using substantial proportionality, continued expansion, or full accommodation because from the factual data stating that none of the institutions complied with the standard of Title IX compliance using the SP test.

Also from the findings, the second recommendation would call for the institutional leaders to implement a three-year study that will give an in-depth understanding of complying with the requirement of Title IX according to the students' interest in athletics at their institution; 100% of the athletic directors perceived that this strategy would be effective or somewhat effective toward complying with Title IX.

The third recommendation would be for the institutional leaders to implement a gender equity committee; the study revealed that 29% of the athletic directors did not know that their institution had a committee or 42% stated that their institution did not have a committee in place to address gender equity and Title IX compliance.

From the practical aspect for the athletic directors, the final recommendation from the researcher would be that the athletic directors receive a thorough understanding of Title IX compliance. This recommendation is offered because for 9 of the 12 items on the survey pertaining to perceptions of Title IX compliance, at least one athletic director indicated that he or she did not know the answer to the question.

**Research Recommendations**

While the present study provided results that can be immediately beneficial to leaders at the public community and junior colleges in Mississippi, it also raised a series of questions that deserve further investigation. To fully examine the potential benefits of Title IX, it is recommended that a study be administered to examine the perception of the student athletes about Title IX's impact on gender equality because the finding suggested that the lack of student interest is the major barrier towards compliance with Title IX according to majority of the athletic directors.

The findings suggested that majority of the athletic directors perceived that creating assistant coaching position would help towards compliance; therefore the second recommendation would call for further research to address the perception of coaches about Title IX's impact on gender equality. Specifically, coaches may have a more personal relationship with the student athletes and could have more insight pertaining to the overall barriers to compliance of Title IX.

Furthermore, the third recommendation would call for further research to elaborate on the specific strategies and barriers toward Title IX compliance identified in the present study. Specific areas such the lack of student interest because of life priorities, redistributing existing athletic budget dollars, insufficient numbers of full-time coaching positions for female sports, and lack of community/region support for female athletic programs would be beneficial. Research of this nature could be used to address why these areas, either perceived or real, exist and could be potentially valid approaches towards complying with the requirements of Title IX.

The researcher would also recommend looking at enrollments of full-time students from online to students actually being on campus; a study should be address pertaining to online full-time students being a factor for institutions being out of compliance. A study on continued expansion prong for Title IX compliance should also be done because majority of the institutions used this test to comply with Title IX according to the athletic directors at a rate of 56%.

The final recommendation would call for a follow-up study for the present research due to the low response rate of the athletic directors.

REFERENCES

Acosta, V., & Carpenter, L. (1992). As the years go by: Coaching opportunities in the 1990s. *Journal of Physical Education, Recreation, and Dance, 63(3),* 36-41.

Agthe, D., & Billings, R. B. (2000). The role of football profits in meeting Title IX gender equity regulations and policy. *Journal of Sports Management, 14,* 28-40.

Airasian, P., & Gay, L. R. (2003). *Educational research: Competencies for analysis and application* (7th ed.). Upper Saddle River, NJ: Person Education Inc.

Airasian, P., Gay, L. R., & Mills, G. E. (2006). *Educational research: Competencies for analysis and application* (8th ed.). Upper Saddle River, NJ: Person Education Inc.

Alexander, B. (2009). *A descriptive study of intercollegiate athletics in Mississippi's public community and junior colleges.* (Doctoral dissertation). Available from ProQuest Dissertations and Theses database. (UMI No. 3386302)

Almond, J., & Cohen. D. (2005). Navigating into the new "safe harbor" model interest surveys as a tool for Title IX compliance programs. *Vanderbilt Journal of Entertainment and Technology Law, 8(1),* 1-43.

American Association of Community Colleges. (2012). *American association of community college.* Retrieved from http://www2.aacc.nche.edu/research/index.htm

Anderson, D. J., & Cheslock, J. J. (2004). Institutional strategies to achieve gender equity in intercollegiate athletics: Does Title IX harm male athletes? *American Economic Review, 94(2),* 307-311.

Anderson, D., Cheslock, J., & Ehrenberg, R. (2006). Gender equity in intercollegiate athletics: Determinants of Title IX compliance. *Journal of Higher Education, 77(2),* 225-260.

Ball, M. (2006). *A comparison of gender equity at institutions with a female athletic director versus institutions with a male athletic director.* (Master's thesis). Available from ProQuest Dissertations and Theses database. (UMI No. 1432740)

Bartlett, K., & Kennedy, R. (1992). *Feminist legal theory: Reading in law and gender.* Boulder, CO: Westview Press.

Beam, M., Faddis, B., & Ruzicka, P. (2004). *Title IX athletics compliance at California's public high schools, community colleges, and universities.* (California Postsecondary Education Commission Rep. 04-04). Sacramento, CA: California Postsecondary Education Commission. RMC Research Corporation. Retrieved from http://www.cpec.ca.gov/completerepors/2004reports/04-04.pdf

Brawer, F. B., & Cohen, A. M. (2003). *The American community college.* (4th ed.). San Francisco, CA: Jossey-Bass.

Brake, D. (2001). The struggle for sex equality in sport and the theory behind Title IX. *University of Michigan Journal of Law Reform, 34(1 & 2).*

Bridges, F., & Roquemore, L. (2004). *Management for athletic/sport administration: theory and practice* (4th ed.). Decatur, GA: Educational Services for Management Books.

Burgess, C. (2006). *Perception of selected community college presidents regarding certain aspects of intercollegiate athletics.* (Doctoral dissertation). Available from ProQuest Dissertation and Theses database. (UMI No. 3215459)

Burnett, S. (2003). Revolution number IX. *Community College Week.* Retrieved from http://www.thefreelibrary.com/Revolution+number+IX.-a0103799478

Byers, W. (1995). *Unsportsmanlike conduct.* Ann Arbor, MI: The University of Michigan Press.

Campbell, C. (2010). *Identifying sports participation opportunities and factors that predict Title IX compliance.* (Doctoral dissertation). Available from ProQuest Dissertations and Theses database. (UMI No. 3215459)

Carpenter, L. J., & Acosta, R. V. (2004). *Women in intercollegiate sport: a longitudinal, national study, twenty-seven year update, 1977-2004.* Retrieved from http://webpages.charter.net/womeninsport?AcostaCarp_2004pdf

Carpenter, L. J., & Acosta, R. V. (2005). *Title IX.* Champaign, IL: Human Kinetics.

Castaneda, C. (2004). *A national overview of intercollegiate athletics in public community colleges.* (Doctoral dissertation). Available from ProQuest Dissertations and Theses database. (UMI No. 3144975)

Causby, C. (2010). *Title IX compliance at two year colleges: An analysis of perceived barriers and strategies.* (Doctoral dissertation). Available from ProQuest Dissertations and Theses database. (UMI No. 3409488)

Cheslock, J., & Eckes, S. (2008). Statistical evidence and compliance with Title IX. *New Directions for Institutional Research, 138,* 31-45.

Cook, S. (2010). Most college coaches don't understand Title IX women in higher education. *Women in Higher Education, 19(12),* 31.

Cohen, D. (2005). *Gender equity in intercollegiate athletics: Where does Pennsylvania stand?* Philadelphia, PA: Women's Law Project.

Compton, N., Compton, J., Dawe, L., & Dawe, J. (2007). Collegiate athletic opportunities for women under Title IX raises the proportionality concern for men's sports. *Journal of Diversity Management, 2(2),* 25-35.

DeHass, D. (2008). *2005-2006 NCAA gender equity report.* Retrieved from http://www.ncaa.org

DeSensi, J., & Rosenberg, D. (2003). *Ethics and morality in sport management.* Morgantown, WV: Fitness Information Technology.

Eckes, S., & Chamberlin, M. (2003). *Title IX and women's athletic opportunities in Indiana colleges and universities.* Bloomington, IN: Indiana Education Policy Center.

Fatheree, B. (2012). *The community and junior college system in Mississippi: A brief history of its origin and development.* Retrieved from http://mshistorynow.mdah.state.ms.us/articles/333/the-community-and-junior-college-system-in-mississippi

Gavora, J. (2002). *Tilting the playing field: schools, sports, sex and Title IX.* San Francisco, CA: Encounter Books.

Gerber, E. W. (1979). The legal basis for the regulation of intercollegiate sport. *Education Record, 60(4),* 467-481.

Greendorfer, S. L. (1989). Catch the vision: Future directions for women in sport. *Journal of Physical Education, Recreation, and Dance, 60(3),* 31-32.

Grant, C. H. (1989). Recapturing the vision. *Journal of Physical Education, Recreation, and Dance, 60(3),* 44-48.

Hoffman, J. L. (2010, November). *Gender equity to American intercollegiate athletics.* Paper presented at the Association for the Study of Higher Education, Indianapolis, IN.

Hunter, R. (2012). The power of feminist judgment? *Feminist Legal Studies, 20(2),* 135-148.

Inglis, S. (2000). *Multiple realities of women's work experiences in coaching and athletic management.* Women in Sports and Physical Activity. Farmington Hills, MI: Gale Group.

Integrated Postsecondary Education Data System. (2012). *Enrollment information.* Retrieved from http://nces.ed.gov/ipeds/

Lamber, J. (2000). Gender and intercollegiate athletics: Data and myths. *University of Michigan Journal of Law Reform, 34(1),* 151-229.

LaNoue, G. R. (1976). Athletics and equality: How to comply with Title IX without tearing down the stadium. *Change, 9(10),* 27-30, 63-64.

Lichtman, B. (1997). Playing fair: What school leaders need to know about Title IX and gender discrimination in athletic programs? *The American School Board Journal, 184(8),* 27.

Lipka, S. (2007). Fresno State grapples with a spate of sex discrimination claims. *The Chronicle of Higher Education. 53(48),* A29.

Mississippi Association of Community and Junior Colleges. (2007). *The Mississippi public community and junior college story: 1972-2002.* Jackson, MS: University Press of Mississippi.

Mumford, V. (1998). *Teams on paper: Title IX compliance in the Maryland junior college athletic conference.* (Doctoral dissertation). Retrieved from http://library.villanova.edu/Find?Summon?Record?od=FETCH-proquest_dll_7328639711

Mumford, V. (2005). A look at women's participation in sports in Maryland two year colleges. *The Sport Journal.* Retrieved from http://www.thesportjournal.org/article/look-womens-participation-sports-maryland-two-year-colleges

Mumford, V. (2006). Promoting equity and access in two year college intercollegiate athletic programs. *Community College Journal of Research and Practice, 30,* 213-222.

National Women's Law Center. (2002). *The battle for gender equity in athletics: Title IX at thirty.* Washington, DC: National Women's Law Center.

Parente, J. (2008). *Student athlete's perceptions of Title IX compliance.* (Doctoral dissertation). Available from ProQuest Dissertations and Theses database. (UMI No. 3336105)

Passeggi, T. (2002). *Title IX and gender equity in intercollegiate athletics: Is it time for a change?* Retrieved from http://law.uoregon.edu/faculty/cforell/docs/titleix.pdf

Paule, A. (2004). *Community perceptions of Title IX.* (Master's thesis). Available from ProQuest Dissertations and Theses database (UMI No. 1421099)

Pelak, C. (2008). The relationship between sexist naming practices and athletic opportunities at colleges and universities in the southern United States, *Sociology of Education, 81(2),* 189-210.

Rosner, S., & Shropshire, K. (2004). *The business of sports.* Sudbury, MA: Jones and Bartlett Publishers.

Schneider, R., Stier, W., Henry, T., & Wilding, G. (2010). Title IX compliance in NCAA athletic departments: Perceptions of senior woman administrators. *Journal of Human Kinetics, 23,* 103-113.

Setty, S. (1993). Leveling the playing field: Reforming the office for Civil Rights to achieve better Title IX enforcement. *Columbia Journal of Law, 32,* 331,355.

Staurowsky, E. (2009). Gender equity in two year athletic departments: Part I. *New Directions for Community Colleges, 147,* 53-62.

Stafford, S. (2004). Progress toward Title IX compliance: The effect of formal and informal enforcement mechanism. *Social Science Quarterly, 85(5),* 1469-1486.

State Board for Community and Junior College. (2012). *Member colleges.* Retrieved from http://www.sbcjc.cc.ms.us

United States Department of Education. (2009). *Equity in athletic disclosure act survey. 2007-2008.* Retrieved from http://ope.ed.gov/athletics

United States Department of Education. (2012). *Equity in athletic disclosure act survey 2010-2011.* Retrieved from http://ope.ed.gov/athletics

United States Department of Justice. (2001). *Title IX legal manual.* Washington, DC:

Civil Right Division of the United States Department of Justice.

Vest, B. & Masterson, G. (2007). Title IX and its effect on sports programs in high school and collegiate athletics. *Coach and Athletic Director, 4*, 60-64.

Videon, T. (2002). Who plays and who benefits: Gender, interscholastic athletics, and academic outcomes. *Sociological Perspective, 45(4)*, 415-444.

Ward, R. (2004). Are doors being opened for the "ladies" of college sports? A covariance analysis. *Sex Roles, 51(11/12)*, 697-708.

Webster. (2007). *Webster's new explorer college dictionary*. Springfield, MA: Federal Street Press.

Young J. M., & Ewing, J. B. (1978). *The Mississippi junior college story: The first fifty years, 1922-1971*. Jackson, MS: University Press of Mississippi.

APPENDIX A

SURVEY APPROVAL LETTER

**From:** Roderick Daniel [mailto:rvd11@msstate.edu]
**Sent:** Tuesday, September 18, 2012 12:10 PM
**To:** Cory Causby
**Subject:** Dissertation approval letter for use of your survey

Cory,

I hope all is well; I am close to finishing. I defend my dissertation next week. However, the email account that you sent your approval letter to me was closed down and re opened and all my emails were lost;if you could write me an approval letter to use your survey that would be great and thank you for everything.

Roderick

Dissertation focus is the Perceptions of Title IX's Impact on gender equity within Intercollegiate athletics: The Mississippi public community and junior colleges

On Tue, Sep 18, 2012 at 11:45 AM, Cory Causby <causby@email.wcu.edu> wrote:

Hi Roderick,

Good to hear from you and congratulations on nearing the completion of your doctoral work. Best of luck to you on your defense.

Please consider this email as my permission for you to utilize my survey for the purposes of your dissertation.

Please let me know if I can provide any additional information and I look forward to checking out your dissertation when it is published.

Thanks,

Cory

APPENDIX B

TWO YEAR INSTITUTION TITLE IX SURVEY

# Two Year Institution Title IX Survey

Answer to this questionnaire will be held in strict confidence and data will be compiled and reported in aggregate for only. Thank you for your sincerity when considering these topics.

**Section 1 - Demographic Data**

Please supply the requested information.

Your personal information will be kept confidential and used only for aggregate analysis. Number of years as an athletic administrator at your current institution:

- 5 or fewer years (1)
- 6 - 10 years (2)
- 11 - 15 years (3)
- 16 - 20 years (4)
- 21 - 25 years (5)
- 26 - or more years (6)

Number of years as an athletic administrator at the two-year college level including your current position:

- 5 or fewer years (1)
- 6 - 10 years (2)
- 11 - 15 years (3)
- 16 - 20 years (4)
- 21 - 25 years (5)
- 26 or more years (6)

Your Gender:

- Male (1)
- Female (2)

Please provide some background information about your institution and athletic programs. Your responses will remain confidential.

How long has your institution participated in intercollegiate athletics?

- ○ 10 years or less (1)
- ○ 11 to 20 years (2)
- ○ 21 to 30 years (3)
- ○ 31 to 40 years (4)
- ○ More than 40 years (5)

How would you describe your President's role in athletics?

- ○ Very Active and involved (1)
- ○ Supportive (2)
- ○ Indifferent (3)
- ○ Restrictive (4)
- ○ Other (5) _____

Which of the three parts of prongs does your institution use to measure Title IX compliance? (select all that apply)

- ❑ Substantial Proportionality (1)
- ❑ Full Accommodation (2)
- ❑ Continued Expansion (3)
- ❑ I Don't Know (4)

## Section II - Level of Title IX Compliance

The following questions assess the compliance to Title IX legislation within the athletic programs at your institution. Please select the answer that best represents your response to each statement. All Information will remain confidential and used only for aggregate analysis.

Elements of Title IX Compliance

| | Yes (1) | No (2) | I Don't Know (3) |
|---|---|---|---|
| A gender appropriate language policy is in place (1) | ○ | ○ | ○ |
| The promotion of gender equity is a priority of the institution (2) | ○ | ○ | ○ |
| All athletic staff are familiar with and understand their responsibilities regarding Title IX compliance (3) | ○ | ○ | ○ |
| A gender equity committee has been formed (4) | ○ | ○ | ○ |
| The sports interests of the student body have been formally evaluated (5) | ○ | ○ | ○ |
| A history and continuing practice of program expansion responsive to developing interests and abilities of members of the under-represented gender exists (6) | ○ | ○ | ○ |
| Current sports offerings fully accommodate the interests and abilities of the institutions | ○ | ○ | ○ |

| | | | |
|---|---|---|---|
| students (7) | | | |
| A plan to insure compliance or bring the institution into compliance with Title IX is in place (8) | O | O | O |
| The institution belongs to a conference that has a plan for compliance to Title IX (9) | O | O | O |
| Male and Female athletes are provided the same opportunities and treatment across all areas of the athletic program (10) | O | O | O |
| The athletic program at my institution is in compliance with Title IX of the Education Amendments Act of 1972 (11) | O | O | O |
| Athletic participation opportunities for students are proportionate to overall female and male enrollments (12) | O | O | O |

## Section III - Strategies Toward Compliance with Title IX

Please indicate how effective you feel each of the following strategies is or would be in strengthening Title IX compliance efforts within your institution's respective athletic program. Select the answer that best represents your response to each strategy. Your response options are: Not Effective, Somewhat Effective, Effective, and Very Effective.

Strategies Toward Title IX Compliance

| | Not Effective (1) | Somewhat Effective (2) | Effective (3) | Very Effective (4) |
|---|---|---|---|---|
| An in-depth evaluation of Title IX compliance within the athletic department (1) | O | O | O | O |
| Add an intercollegiate sport and its head coach position for women (2) | O | O | O | O |
| Add a varsity head coach to alleviate current coaching staff overload (3) | O | O | O | O |
| Create a full time assistant coach position for women to assist the current coaching staff (4) | O | O | O | O |
| Redistribute existing athletic budget dollars (5) | O | O | O | O |
| Invest special funds into the budget of the under-financed | O | O | O | O |

| | | | | |
|---|---|---|---|---|
| sports to enhance the number and quality of opportunities (6) | | | | |
| Emphasize growth of participation by women in sports with large participation potential (e.g. swimming, soccer, track and field, cross country) (7) | O | O | O | O |
| Fund the development and implementation of a plan to control attrition on women's teams (8) | O | O | O | O |
| Reduce the number of sports available to men (9) | O | O | O | O |
| Limit squad sizes in sports for men (10) | O | O | O | O |
| Encourage a conference-wide standard of compliance to Title IX (11) | O | O | O | O |
| Fund out-reach programs for women to encourage involvement in sport activity (12) | O | O | O | O |
| Encourage the | O | O | O | O |

| | | | | |
|---|---|---|---|---|
| filing of formal grievances in the areas of non-compliance to Title IX in the athletic programs with the Title IX officer on campus (13) | | | | |
| Create a full-time administrative position to oversee Women's athletics programs (14) | ○ | ○ | ○ | ○ |
| Other (1) (15) | ○ | ○ | ○ | ○ |
| Other (2) (16) | ○ | ○ | ○ | ○ |

## Section IV - Barriers to Title IX Compliance

Please indicate your level of agreement or disagreement with the following statements pertaining to barriers to Title IX compliance faced by your colleges and athletic program. Select the response which best represents your agreement with each of the following statements.

Barriers to Title IX Compliance

| | Strongly Disagree (1) | Disagree (2) | Agree (3) | Strongly Agree (4) |
|---|---|---|---|---|
| The attitude of administrative superiors limits growth of athletics opportunities for women (1) | ○ | ○ | ○ | ○ |
| The attitude of administrative superiors that there are not equal numbers across gender of skilled athletes to participate in inter-collegiate sports (2) | ○ | ○ | ○ | ○ |
| Insufficient numbers of women in athletic leadership positions (3) | ○ | ○ | ○ | ○ |
| Insufficient numbers of female coaches in athletic department (4) | ○ | ○ | ○ | ○ |
| Insufficient numbers o full-time coaching positions for female sports (5) | ○ | ○ | ○ | ○ |
| Lack of student interest because of other life priorities (6) | ○ | ○ | ○ | ○ |
| Lack of community/region support for female athletic programs (7) | ○ | ○ | ○ | ○ |
| Inability to attract | ○ | ○ | ○ | ○ |

| | | | | |
|---|---|---|---|---|
| women into current athletic programs (8) | | | | |
| Inability to retain women in athletic program (9) | ○ | ○ | ○ | ○ |
| A finite number of budget dollars causes a reaction to protect present budgets, thus limiting support for growth in programs for women (10) | ○ | ○ | ○ | ○ |
| Different/unequal institutional funding models for athletics programs (11) | ○ | ○ | ○ | ○ |
| External support and financial resources (booster club, fund raising) are not available to programs across gender (12) | ○ | ○ | ○ | ○ |
| Unequal facilities (locker rooms, offices, practice space) (13) | ○ | ○ | ○ | ○ |
| Unequal/unavailable financial support to recruit female (14) | ○ | ○ | ○ | ○ |
| A socialization process in the United States which does not promote the participation of both genders in sport to the same extent (15) | ○ | ○ | ○ | ○ |
| An overall lack of understanding of Title IX compliance regulations (16) | ○ | ○ | ○ | ○ |
| Lack of centralized conference/association level training and | ○ | ○ | ○ | ○ |

| | | | | |
|---|---|---|---|---|
| compliance programs available (17) | | | | |
| Title IX regulations do not account for differences between two and four-year athletic programs (18) | ○ | ○ | ○ | ○ |
| Current Title IX legislation is not effective in ensuring gender equity in intercollegiate athletics at the two-year college level (19) | ○ | ○ | ○ | ○ |
| Other (1) (20) | ○ | ○ | ○ | ○ |
| Other (2) (21) | ○ | ○ | ○ | ○ |

APPENDIX C

IRB APPROVAL LETTER

July 16, 2012

Roderick Daniel
207 Forrest Street
Aberdeen, MS 39730

RE: IRB Study #12-225: Perceptions of Title IX's Impact on Gender Equity within Intercollegiate Athletics: The Mississippi Public Community and Junior Colleges

Dear Mr. Daniel:

This email serves as official documentation that the above referenced project was reviewed and approved via administrative review on 7/16/2012 in accordance with 45 CFR 46.101(b)(2). Continuing review is not necessary for this project. However, any modification to the project must be reviewed and approved by the IRB prior to implementation. Any failure to adhere to the approved protocol could result in suspension or termination of your project. The IRB reserves the right, at anytime during the project period, to observe you and the additional researchers on this project.

**Please note that the MSU IRB is in the process of seeking accreditation for our human subjects protection !program. As a result of these efforts, you will likely notice many changes in the IRB's policies and procedures in the coming months. These changes will be posted online at http://www.orc.msstate.edu/human/aahrpp.php. The first of these changes is the implementation of an approval stamp for consent forms. The approval stamp will assist in ensuring the IRB approved version of the consent form is used in the actual conduct of research. Your stamped consent form will be attached in a separate email. The consent form must either be an attachment to the recruitment email or the wording must be on the first screen of the online survey.**

Please refer to your IRB number (#12-225) when contacting our office regarding this application.

Thank you for your cooperation and good luck to you in conducting this research project. If you have questions or concerns, please contact me at cwilliams@research.msstate.edu or call 662-325-5220. In addition, we would greatly appreciate your feedback on the IRB approval process. Please take a few minutes to complete our survey at http://www.surveymonkey.com/s/YZC7QQD.

Sincerely,

Christine Williams, MPPA, CIP
IRB Compliance Administrator

cc: Debra Prince

www.ingramcontent.com/pod-product-compliance
Lightning Source LLC
Chambersburg PA
CBHW030906180526
45163CB00004B/1733